™

MW00680759

Certification for the Rest of Us! ™

BESTSELLING BOOK SERIES FROM IDG

Are you intimidated and confused by computers? Do you find that traditional manuals are overloaded with technical details you'll never use? Do your friends and family always call you to fix simple problems on their PCs? Then the *...For Dummies®* computer book series from IDG Books Worldwide is for you.

...For Dummies books are written for those frustrated computer users who know they aren't really dumb but find that PC hardware, software, and indeed the unique vocabulary of computing make them feel helpless. *...For Dummies* books use a lighthearted approach, a down-to-earth style, and even cartoons and humorous icons to diffuse computer novices' fears and build their confidence. Lighthearted but not lightweight, these books are a perfect survival guide for anyone forced to use a computer.

Already, millions of satisfied readers agree. They have made *...For Dummies* books the #1 introductory level computer book series and have written asking for more. So, if you're looking for the most fun and easy way to learn about computers, look to *...For Dummies* books to give you a helping hand.

™

IDG BOOKS
WORLDWIDE

MCSE
STUDY TIPS
FOR
DUMMIES®

by Curt Simmons and Patrick Terrance Neal

IDG Books Worldwide, Inc.
An International Data Group Company

Foster City, CA ♦ Chicago, IL ♦ Indianapolis, IN ♦ New York, NY

MCSE Study Tips For Dummies®

Published by
IDG Books Worldwide, Inc.
An International Data Group Company
919 E. Hillsdale Blvd.
Suite 400
Foster City, CA 94404
www.idgbooks.com (IDG Books Worldwide Web site)
www.dummies.com (Dummies Press Web site)

Library of Congress Catalog Card No.: 98-87912

ISBN: 0-7645-0484-3

Printed in the United States of America

10 9 8 7 6 5 4 3 2 1

1B/RV/RS/ZY/IN

Distributed in the United States by IDG Books Worldwide, Inc.

Distributed by Macmillan Canada for Canada; by Transworld Publishers Limited in the United Kingdom; by IDG Norge Books for Norway; by IDG Sweden Books for Sweden; by Woodslane Pty. Ltd. for Australia; by Woodslane (NZ) Ltd. for New Zealand; by Addison Wesley Longman Singapore Pte Ltd. for Singapore, Malaysia, Thailand, and Indonesia; by Norma Comunicaciones S.A. for Colombia; by Intersoft for South Africa; by International Thomson Publishing for Germany, Austria and Switzerland; by Distribuidora Cuspide for Argentina; by Livraria Cultura for Brazil; by Ediciencia S.A. for Ecuador; by Ediciones ZETA S.C.R. Ltda. for Peru; by WS Computer Publishing Corporation, Inc., for the Philippines; by Contemporanea de Ediciones for Venezuela; by Express Computer Distributors for the Caribbean and West Indies; by Micronesia Media Distributor, Inc. for Micronesia; by Grupo Editorial Norma S.A. for Guatemala; by Chips Computadoras S.A. de C.V. for Mexico; by Editorial Norma de Panama S.A. for Panama; by Wouters Import for Belgium; by American Bookshops for Finland. Authorized Sales Agent: Anthony Rudkin Associates for the Middle East and North Africa.

For general information on IDG Books Worldwide's books in the U.S., please call our Consumer Customer Service department at 800-762-2974. For reseller information, including discounts and premium sales, please call our Reseller Customer Service department at 800-434-3422.

For information on where to purchase IDG Books Worldwide's books outside the U.S., please contact our International Sales department at 317-596-5530 or fax 317-596-5692.

For information on foreign language translations, please contact our Foreign & Subsidiary Rights department at 650-655-3021 or fax 650-655-3281.

For sales inquiries and special prices for bulk quantities, please contact our Sales department at 650-655-3200 or write to the address above.

For information on using IDG Books Worldwide's books in the classroom or for ordering examination copies, please contact our Educational Sales department at 800-434-2086 or fax 317-596-5499.

For press review copies, author interviews, or other publicity information, please contact our Public Relations department at 650-655-3000 or fax 650-655-3299.

For authorization to photocopy items for corporate, personal, or educational use, please contact Copyright Clearance Center, 222 Rosewood Drive, Danvers, MA 01923, or fax 978-750-4470.

is a trademark under exclusive license to IDG Books Worldwide, Inc., from International Data Group, Inc.

About the Authors

Curt Simmons, MCSE, MCT, is a freelance writer and Microsoft technical trainer from Dallas, Texas. His primary focus is Windows operating systems and Internet software. In addition to his MCSE and MCT certifications, Curt has a master's degree in education. When he is not writing and training, he enjoys the great outdoors and spending time with his 2-year-old daughter, Hannah.

Patrick Terrance Neal, MCSE, MCT, is an independent contractor and consultant from Tampa, Florida. In addition to his computer consulting work, Patrick teaches seminars on how to study for the MCSE certification exams.

ABOUT IDG BOOKS WORLDWIDE

Welcome to the world of IDG Books Worldwide.

IDG Books Worldwide, Inc., is a subsidiary of International Data Group, the world's largest publisher of computer-related information and the leading global provider of information services on information technology. IDG was founded more than 30 years ago by Patrick J. McGovern and now employs more than 9,000 people worldwide. IDG publishes more than 290 computer publications in over 75 countries. More than 90 million people read one or more IDG publications each month.

Launched in 1990, IDG Books Worldwide is today the #1 publisher of best-selling computer books in the United States. We are proud to have received eight awards from the Computer Press Association in recognition of editorial excellence and three from Computer Currents' First Annual Readers' Choice Awards. Our best-selling ...For Dummies® series has more than 50 million copies in print with translations in 31 languages. IDG Books Worldwide, through a joint venture with IDG's Hi-Tech Beijing, became the first U.S. publisher to publish a computer book in the People's Republic of China. In record time, IDG Books Worldwide has become the first choice for millions of readers around the world who want to learn how to better manage their businesses.

Our mission is simple: Every one of our books is designed to bring extra value and skill-building instructions to the reader. Our books are written by experts who understand and care about our readers. The knowledge base of our editorial staff comes from years of experience in publishing, education, and journalism — experience we use to produce books to carry us into the new millennium. In short, we care about books, so we attract the best people. We devote special attention to details such as audience, interior design, use of icons, and illustrations. And because we use an efficient process of authoring, editing, and desktop publishing our books electronically, we can spend more time ensuring superior content and less time on the technicalities of making books.

You can count on our commitment to deliver high-quality books at competitive prices on topics you want to read about. At IDG Books Worldwide, we continue in the IDG tradition of delivering quality for more than 30 years. You'll find no better book on a subject than one from IDG Books Worldwide.

John Kilcullen
Chairman and CEO
IDG Books Worldwide, Inc.

Steven Berkowitz
President and Publisher
IDG Books Worldwide, Inc.

*Eighth Annual
Computer Press
Awards ≥1992*

*Ninth Annual
Computer Press
Awards ≥1993*

*Tenth Annual
Computer Press
Awards ≥1994*

*Eleventh Annual
Computer Press
Awards ≥1995*

Dedication

We dedicate this book to the many people who offered us informal "MCSE study tips" while we were working on our certifications. In a great sense, they paved the way for us to put this book in your hands!

Authors' Acknowledgments

This book would not have been possible without the extraordinary efforts of John Pont — you deserve a medal, John! We would like to offer a special thank you to Sherri Morningstar and Joyce Pepple at IDG Books, for their faith and encouragement during this project. Linda Stark, copy editor for this book, gets a big thanks for her insights and her careful attention to detail. Thanks to Margot Maley, our literary agent, for working out all the details. Also, thanks to Scott Rachui, technical reviewer, who kept us honest and offered valuable suggestions from his own MCSE study experience.

Publisher's Acknowledgments

We're proud of this book; please register your comments through our IDG Books Worldwide Online Registration Form located at http://my2cents.dummies.com.

Some of the people who helped bring this book to market include the following:

Acquisitions, Editorial, and Media Development

Project Editor: John W. Pont

Acquisitions Editors: Jill Pisoni, Sherri Morningstar, Joyce Pepple

Copy Editor: Linda S. Stark

Technical Editor: Scott Rachui

Associate Permissions Editor: Carmen Krikorian

Editorial Manager: Mary C. Corder

Media Development Manager: Heather Heath Dismore

Editorial Assistant: Alison Walthall

Production

Project Coordinator: Karen York

Layout and Graphics: Daniel Alexander, Lou Boudreau, Maridee V. Ennis, Angela F. Hunckler, Jane E. Martin, Brent Savage, Jacque Schneider, Brian Torwelle

Proofreaders: Kelli Botta, Henry Lazarek, Rebecca Senninger, Ethel M. Winslow

Indexer: Sharon Hilgenberg

Special Help

Paula Lowell, Suzanne Thomas

General and Administrative

IDG Books Worldwide, Inc.: John Kilcullen, CEO; Steven Berkowitz, President and Publisher

IDG Books Technology Publishing: Brenda McLaughlin, Senior Vice President and Group Publisher

Dummies Technology Press and Dummies Editorial: Diane Graves Steele, Vice President and Associate Publisher; Mary Bednarek, Director of Acquisitions and Product Development; Kristin A. Cocks, Editorial Director

Dummies Trade Press: Kathleen A. Welton, Vice President and Publisher; Kevin Thornton, Acquisitions Manager

IDG Books Production for Dummies Press: Michael R. Britton, Vice President of Production and Creative Services; Cindy L. Phipps, Manager of Project Coordination, Production Proofreading, and Indexing; Kathie S. Schutte, Supervisor of Page Layout; Shelley Lea, Supervisor of Graphics and Design; Debbie J. Gates, Production Systems Specialist; Robert Springer, Supervisor of Proofreading; Debbie Stailey, Special Projects Coordinator; Tony Augsburger, Supervisor of Reprints and Bluelines

Dummies Packaging and Book Design: Robin Seaman, Creative Director; Kavish + Kavish, Cover Design

◆

The publisher would like to give special thanks to Patrick J. McGovern, without whom this book would not have been possible.

◆

Contents at a Glance

Cartoons at a Glance

By Rich Tennant

"Can't I just give you riches or something?"

page 7

"He studies every available minute for his MCSE exam."

page 89

"We sort of have our own way of mentally preparing our people to take an MCSE exam."

page 45

page 125

"...and it doesn't appear that you'll have much trouble grasping some of the more 'alien' configuration concepts on this MCSE exam."

page 157

Fax: 978-546-7747 • E-mail: the5wave@tiac.net

Table of Contents

. . . .

Introduction

*I*n today's job market, demand for people with the MCSE (Microsoft Certified Systems Engineer) certification far exceeds the supply. And this demand shows no signs of stopping, not even into the next century. For systems professionals who want to enhance their positions in the information technology field, Microsoft certifications are indeed the hottest ticket around!

Whether you've already decided to pursue the MCSE certification or are just curious about the certification process, you're in the right place. *MCSE Study Tips For Dummies* is much more than a study guide. This book guides you through the whole certification process, from the decision to pursue MCSE certification to the last exam you take on the road to earning those coveted initials. You can find a practice exam, analysis of exam questions, and methods to improve your studying and test-taking skills. We can't promise that you'll have cleaner, brighter teeth, but we can help to smooth the sometimes bumpy path to MCSE certification.

About This Book

Studying for an MCSE exam is especially challenging, requiring a particular set of skills. Taking an MCSE exam is just as formidable. Both tasks require that you reach far beyond the comfortable limits of your abilities. The MCSE certification process is a unique experience, and regardless of your current abilities, your first MCSE exam is bound to surprise you if you're not prepared. The great thing about skills, however, is that you can develop them. Moreover, if you follow the advice that we offer in this book, you can count on acquiring the know-how you need for passing the MCSE exams.

Before you begin studying, however, you must understand the MCSE certification *process*. You don't pursue MCSE certification by simply getting a course catalog and signing up for classes as you would in a traditional university. When you begin the MCSE certification process, you are immediately confronted with questions, such as:

- Which exams do I take to become certified?
- Do I need to attend classroom training to prepare for the exams?
- What kinds of questions can I expect to see on the exams?

✔ Where and how do I take the exams?

✔ How much do the certification exams cost?

✔ How do I pay for them?

Making your way through all the questions and considerations — and responding in a way that's right for you — is a forbidding process. In most cases, no one stands ready to guide you through it all. That's why we wrote this book.

You won't find a more concise guide to the MCSE certification process. *MCSE Study Tips For Dummies* answers your questions quickly and directly, so that you can get on with what's important — namely, preparing for and passing the MCSE exams.

MCSE Study Tips For Dummies guides you through the MCSE certification process, acquainting you with study strategies, question styles, and test-taking techniques. However, you won't find exam-specific information in this book. For all the details about what to expect on a specific exam, you need to dig into a copy of the appropriate *MCSE ...For Dummies* book.

Each exam-specific *MCSE ...For Dummies* book tells you precisely what you need to know — as well as what you don't need to know — for a particular exam. For example, *MCSE Windows NT Server 4 in the Enterprise For Dummies* gives you the complete lowdown on Exam 70-068, Implementing and Supporting Windows NT Server 4.0 in the Enterprise. Each of those exam-specific books provides a wealth of quick assessment tests, chapter reviews, practice exams, and timesaving tips for succeeding on a particular MCSE certification exam.

MCSE Study Tips For Dummies complements the exam-specific *MCSE ...For Dummies* books by acquainting you with the MCSE and other Microsoft certifications. This book tells you how to earn those certifications, and what they mean to your future.

This book is also a guide to passing the certification exams. We provide a concise listing of Microsoft's exam preparation objectives, and we offer successful strategies for passing the exams.

Throughout this book, we focus on one overriding goal: helping you brave the sometimes rocky, and always twisting, passage to certification.

Foolish Assumptions

We make the following foolish assumptions about everyone reading this book:

✔ You are naturally curious.

✔ You have lots of motivation.

✔ You like to question what people tell you.

Of course, that list may describe just about everyone you've ever worked with in the information technology field.

Most importantly, we assume that you have the drive and the determination to earn MCSE certification. This book can help to guide you through the certification process, but you must understand that achieving MCSE certification requires plenty of effort on your part. Passing the certification exams calls for in-depth knowledge of Microsoft tools and technologies, and you gain that knowledge with hard work and careful study.

We realize that we're writing for a diverse, savvy group of people. However, we also believe that anyone who understands the relevant technologies and has the necessary motivation can use the advice that we offer in this book.

How to Use This Book

You can read *MCSE Study Tips For Dummies* from cover to cover or you can jump around from section to section. You can use any portion of this book as an instant reference source. For example, if you're ready to start taking MCSE exams, you can consult the information we offer on analyzing exam questions.

Or if you need to know how to schedule an exam, you can flip to the appropriate appendix for information. Need some good third-party references? Or perhaps you want to read about your choices among the various certification tracks? No problem! Just check the index and then turn to the pages that cover those topics.

How This Book Is Organized

This book is organized in five parts. The first three parts are designed to guide you through a particular phase of the certification process. This information includes selecting a certification track as well as studying for and taking an exam.

The fourth and fifth parts contain all the other valuable information that doesn't quite fit into the first three parts. This information includes job-hunting tips, a practice exam, and a full listing of Microsoft's exam preparation objectives for the core exams.

Part I: Getting It Together — Options for the MCSE

If you've ever wondered just what the MCSE is, or if you want to know what it costs, Part I unveils a wealth of details. We cram lots of information into the chapters in Part I, including all the MCSE exam choices, certification options, and a realistic discussion of the job market for people who earn MCSE certification.

Part II: The Journey Begins — Studying for Your MCSE

How long has it been since you studied for an exam? Do you just need to brush up on your studying and exam-taking skills, or do you require a full-fledged reintroduction to preparing for and taking a test? Whichever description fits your personal situation, Part II is the place to go to polish up skills — no matter how rusty they are.

Part III: Conquering the MCSE Exams

In Part III, you prepare for the big day — your MCSE certification exams. We explain the intricacies of exam questions and we offer lots of advice for managing the exam. We also give you some suggestions for getting ready on the day of the exam.

We don't want to fill your head with negative thoughts, but Part III also provides some suggestions about facing a no-pass on any exam. Lots of people fail an MCSE exam on the first try, but we can help you turn that unexpected and unpleasant result into a positive learning experience.

Part IV: The Part of Tens

Like all ...*For Dummies* books, this book has a Part of Tens, which imparts loads of valuable information. We pack lots of helpful advice into Part IV — everything from the most important study tips to remember to Web sites where you can post your resumé after you earn MCSE certification. You don't want to miss the Part of Tens.

Part V: Appendixes

Don't overlook the appendixes in Part V of this book. In Part V, you can find advice for scheduling your MCSE exam, a practice exam, and a complete listing of the exam objectives for the MCSE core exams.

Icons Used in This Book

You see the following icons throughout the pages of *MCSE Study Tips For Dummies*:

The Tip icon highlights general, all-purpose tips and information worth keeping in mind as you head toward exam time.

The Warning icon identifies a high-level alert that should send up flags of suspicion. We often use the Warning icon to highlight advice for avoiding a pitfall that we encountered along the path to MCSE certification.

The Remember icon flags really important information that we want you to burn into your brain.

The Time Shaver icon points out advice that can help you save time when you're studying or taking an MCSE certification exam.

How This Book Can Keep You on Course

Think of this book as a pointer, similar to the cursor on your computer desktop. When you use it, the resources you need are just a click away.

We designed *MCSE Study Tips For Dummies* to answer lots of questions for you and, for those really big puzzlers, to point you in the right direction for reliable, up-to-date information.

And remember, you can always call the MCP Hotline at 800-636-7544. After all, they're the ones with all the answers — right?

Part I

Getting It Together — Options for the MCSE

The 5th Wave   By Rich Tennant

"Can't I just give you riches or something?"

In this part . . .

No matter where you are along the path to becoming an MCSE, Part I is a great place to start exploring. In this part, you take a realistic look at just what Microsoft certification involves, as well as delve into the truths and myths surrounding it. The chapters in Part I describe the various certifications that Microsoft offers, and they list the requirements for earning MCSE certification.

Chapter 1

So You Wanna Be an MCSE?

- -

In This Chapter

▶ Understanding what MCSE certification means

▶ Examining Skills 2000

▶ Exploring the benefits of certification

▶ Assessing the MCSE job market

▶ Determining whether MCSE certification is right for you

▶ Making the commitment to earn certification

- -

With so much information available about the MCSE certification and so many places to look, just the process of gathering information is an overwhelming task. This chapter helps you to avoid MCSE information overload by giving you the lowdown on this certification and what it means to your career in the information technology (IT) field.

In this chapter, we explain what MCSE certification represents, and we discuss Skills 2000, a Microsoft initiative to recruit people for IT careers. We offer some examples of the types of jobs that people with MCSE certification typically perform, and we discuss realistic earnings expectations for people who achieve MCSE certification. Perhaps most importantly, we help you understand the commitment you must make if you decide to pursue MCSE certification.

What Is MCSE Certification Anyway?

The MCSE, or Microsoft Certified Systems Engineer, is a certification offered by Microsoft. To obtain the MCSE certification, you must pass six exams.

Actually, you may be able to get your MCSE certification by passing only five exams. We give you all the details about the requirements for MCSE certification in Chapter 3.

According to Microsoft, earning MCSE certification indicates that you know how to "effectively plan, implement, maintain, and support information systems" using Microsoft products. Of course, you may already perform these tasks, even though you haven't taken any of the certification exams. The MCSE certification simply tells the world that you meet Microsoft's standards for proficiency in performing these tasks.

Earning the designation of MCSE doesn't guarantee anything. Although it's a highly sought after certification, the MCSE, in itself, means only that you passed the exams. You aren't automatically offered the job of your dreams — or even a raise in your current salary. Although recruiters may knock down your door after you claim the certification, you can bet that they'll ask you about real-world experience. Your job prospects and your earning potential depend on your experience *and* your MCSE certification.

Understanding all the fuss about Microsoft certifications

According to the June 1998 issue of *MCP Magazine*, more than 48,000 professionals have earned MCSE certification. By the time you read this book, the demand for MCSEs almost certainly will have pushed that figure even higher.

So why all the fuss about this certification anyway? The computer industry already has more than 48,000 MCSEs . . . Isn't that enough?

Well, no. According to the June 1998 issue of the *Maddux Report*, reporting on a speech by Bill Gates to an Orlando audience, "There are now about 350,000 unfilled IT jobs in the United States, and another million such jobs are likely to be created in the next seven years."

Great demand clearly exists for qualified IT professionals. What's also clear is that the IT industry has lots more jobs than people to fill them.

And just how many MCSEs does the world need? That's hard to say. But 48,000 isn't enough.

 For an informative, honest assessment of the current and projected demand for high-technology career people, read the article that appears on the following page at the Web site of *High Technology Careers Magazine*:

    www.hightechcareers.com/docs/dec-cars.html

As of June 1998, Microsoft had awarded just over 100 MCSE+Internet certifications. (For in-depth descriptions of the MCSE and its various options, see Chapter 2.) Forecasts for Internet commerce are nearly as difficult to pin down as MCSE numbers. But even at a rate of triple or quadruple growth in Internet trade through the beginning of the next century, anybody with an Internet certification is going to do well.

Strong demand exists not only for networking professionals but also for trainers, or MCTs (Microsoft Certified Trainers). As we write this chapter, more than 12,000 people have earned MCT certification. That isn't a lot when you consider that, if Bill Gates is right, at least 350,000 trained personnel are needed just to fill the current demand for IT professionals. Who will train them? That's why Microsoft started Skills 2000, which we discuss later in this chapter. Skills 2000, among other objectives, is scouring the public schools in the United States, seeking the desperately needed instructors.

But don't put the cart before the horse. You must become an MCSE before you can become an MCT. And before you earn MCSE certification, you become an MCP — Microsoft Certified Professional.

For more information about career opportunities for people who have earned MCSE certification, visit www.microsoft.com/mcp/certstep/steps.htm. This site details every step of the certification process, including career potential, from the Microsoft perspective.

MCP — First step to MCSE

After you pass any certification exam (with the exception of Networking Essentials), you become an MCP, or Microsoft Certified Professional. And although this book focuses on the MCSE certification, the goal of some individuals is MCP certification only. Generally, if this is your aim, you are a specialist, seeking certification status in a particular subject matter.

Chapter 2 explores each major certification in detail. Chapter 3 offers the complete scoop on which exams you must pass to earn your MCSE certification.

Regardless of the Microsoft certification you are seeking, you can still benefit from this book. Although exam content changes, Microsoft tests are identical in presentation and style. And even though this book is designed to enable success on MCSE exams, the study and exam-taking skills that we provide in this book apply to any Microsoft certification exam that you may take.

You become an MCP before becoming an MCSE. Confused? Just think of the MCP as the first step — like a high school diploma is necessary before you enter college. Which means that as long as you are an MCSE, you are also an MCP.

If you need to know anything about the MCP program, check out the Microsoft Web site at the following address:

```
www.microsoft.com/mcp/
```

This Web site also has a page for frequently asked questions:

```
www.microsoft.com/mcp/certstep/mcpfaq.htm
```

What is Skills 2000?

Initiated by Microsoft in May 1997, the Skills 2000 program seeks to recruit people for information technology careers. The Skills 2000 program offers

- ✔ **Senior recruitment.** Working with the Green Thumb organization, Microsoft recruits, trains, and places senior citizens in high–tech careers.

- ✔ **Training opportunities for high school students.** Microsoft works at the grass roots level to snare students while they're still in high school. The Authorized Academic Training Partner (AATP) program is devoted to authorizing secondary schools, colleges, and universities to certify individuals. An AATP teaches the same curriculum as an Authorized Technical Education Center, or ATEC.

- ✔ **Loans.** Skills 2000 offers lower-interest rate loans for people who can't afford the cost of training.

- ✔ **Jobs.** Working with The Monster Board (`www.monster.com`), Skills 2000 works to place newly certified MCSEs. Chapter 15 describes the Monster Board and several other Web sites where you can post your resumé.

For complete information about the Skills 2000 program, you can investigate the Skills 2000 Web site:

```
www.microsoft.com/skills2000/
```

This site offers a variety of information, including a skills assessment, descriptions of jobs, and links to MCSE and MCP sites. Figure 1-1 shows the home page for the Skills 2000 Web site.

The Skills 2000 home page offers a good starting point for anyone interested in some preliminary information about high-technology careers. This page also includes a link to *MCP Magazine's* salary survey, as well as a link to Microsoft Certified Solution Providers offering career opportunities.

Review the information at these sites, but don't take any of the salary figures too literally until you check out conditions in your local market.

The Skills 2000 home page has a link called `What is IT?`. Clicking this link takes you to a page of different networking career options. At that page, click the `Network Specialist` link, which takes you to the page shown in Figure 1-2.

The Web page shown in Figure 1-2 provides a general outline of what a network specialist does on the job. In the following section, we list typical job titles and responsibilities for IT positions that may require MCSE certification.

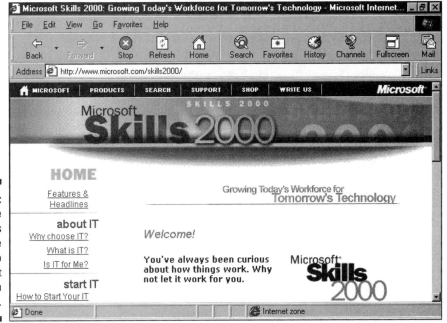

Figure 1-1:
You can use the Skills 2000 home page to start planning an IT career.

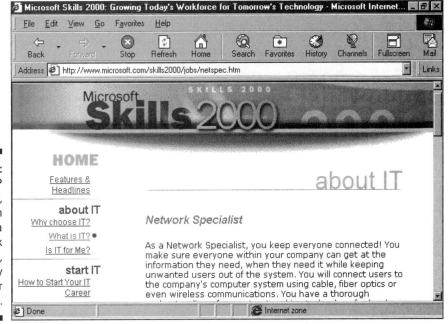

Figure 1-2:
As an MCP or MCSE, you can become a Network Specialist, one of many career options.

What does an MCSE do?

Have you ever wondered about the daily duties of an MCSE? The MCSE certification indicates that you are qualified to work with network information systems using Microsoft products. But how does that description translate to the real world?

If you work for a large company, which for sake of example, we define as 100-plus employees, the following job titles are common for an MCSE:

- Systems Administrator
- Assistant Systems Administrator
- Backup Manager
- Microsoft Exchange Administrator, MS-Mail Postmaster, or E-mail Administrator

In addition, here's a sampling of the most common duties for positions that require MCSE certification:

- Managing segments of a multi-network system
- Serving as project or team leader for system upgrades
- Consulting on planning projects
- Managing user profiles
- Performing backups
- Maintaining network environment security
- Managing a staff of five or more employees
- Providing after-hours, on-call support
- Troubleshooting system problems

For an MCSE working in a small to medium-size company (5 to 100 employees), here are some common duties:

- Planning, maintaining, and troubleshooting network systems
- Consulting on upgrades
- Installing networks and computers
- Setting up entire networks
- Purchasing equipment
- Preparing proposals for network installations
- Laying cables

✔ Installing network printers

✔ Providing after-hours, on-call support for troubleshooting

✔ Troubleshooting system problems

✔ Managing a small staff (two employees or less)

✔ Arranging for end-user training

The preceding lists simply offer examples of common job titles and duties for an MCSE. Numerous positions of varying descriptions and skill levels are available for IT professionals with MCSE certification.

This wealth of opportunities can be a nightmare, however, if you're trying to decide on a career discipline. If you become a systems administrator, you must be a jack-of-all-trades, which is challenging in such a rapidly changing field. On the other hand, you may want to specialize as an MCSE. This objective is easier to accomplish in larger companies, which often need specialized administrators. For example, you may become an Exchange administrator, maintaining a corporate e-mail system, or a Webmaster, working with a company's link to the Internet.

What Are You Expecting from MCSE Certification?

The information technology (IT) industry is changing constantly. Today, you may read that the average salary for an IT professional with MCSE certification is $55,000. Tomorrow, certified IT professionals may command $60,000. Yesterday, the going rate was a mere $45,000. What salary can you expect after you earn MCSE certification?

If you're looking for a book that tells you how to attain MCSE certification in two weeks, without prior experience, so that you can start earning $60,000 a year, then *MCSE Study Tips For Dummies* isn't the resource for you. We don't make promises that your employer may not keep.

We can only tell you that the salary you can expect to command after earning your MCSE certification depends on your experience, your responsibilities, and your location. But you already knew that — right?

Because you already work in the IT industry, the MCSE certification can boost your paycheck as well as your opportunities for advancement. Understanding the benefits of professional certification, your employer may reward you for earning your MCSE credentials.

On the other hand, even with MCSE certification, a newcomer to the IT industry should expect entry-level employment opportunities. Depending on the size of the company, these positions can range from working the help desk to serving as assistant to a technology manager. These jobs offer entry-level IT professionals excellent opportunities to hone their skills before moving on to more advanced and higher-paying positions.

We understand that in some geographic markets, entry-level MCSEs can also find positions managing Information System departments for small companies. These companies are often willing to take an inexperienced person at a lower salary.

We strongly advise that entry-level IT professionals consider these opportunities carefully. A small-company environment offers an excellent chance to learn all aspects of networking. And when you're ready to look for another job, you can add an impressive title to your resumé. However, working in this type of company also can be fast-paced and demanding, both physically and mentally. As the person in charge, you'll be asked to troubleshoot a variety of problems . . . and solve them. If the company's network goes down, your employer won't wait while you take a class to find out how to fix the problem.

Setting realistic salary expectations

Are you ready to make lots of money as an MCSE? Are you hanging on our every word, hoping to find out that as soon as you earn MCSE certification, you'll make $70,000 — or more? Sorry, but it's time for a reality check.

The best way to know what kind of income you can expect after earning MCSE certification is to research salaries in your area. You may make $60,000 if you live in California or New York City. With extensive experience, you may even make $100,000. In Florida, however, you may make from $35,000 to $50,000 with experience.

The important point is to be realistic. Ask around. Compare salaries in your area using various resources such as classifieds, contacts, and personal experience. Discuss the benefits of certification with your employer. Then make your own judgment about what you can realistically expect to earn as an MCSE.

We can't pin down the numbers for you, no matter how hard we try. So be realistic about the salary you expect. Remember, your level of experience plays a big role in determining the salary you can command.

Finding a job as an MCSE

The world can indeed be your oyster if you're an MCSE. Job offers that include signing bonuses and relocation expenses are highly likely — even if you don't have lots of experience. Earning MCSE certification can give you more clout when you're negotiating for those types of perks.

A salary sampling exercise

Here's an exercise that you can do using any Sunday newspaper. Search the classifieds for system administrator jobs, noting the salaries. Write this information down, making sure to note whether the position requires experience or an MCSE certification. Your list should look something like the following example, including exact quotes from the newspaper ads:

- ✔ MCSE candidates, "We'll pay for training," $30,000.

- ✔ MCSE, "6 months experience," $35,000.

- ✔ Systems Administrators, "We'll help you get your MCSE," $40,000.

- ✔ Systems Administrator, "MCSE preferred, 1 to 2 years experience," $45,000.

- ✔ Systems Administrator, "MCSE required, 5+ years experience," $65,000.

Look at the wide range of salaries in this example, from $30,000 to $65,000. That's a $35,000 difference — more than 100 percent — from the lowest to the highest salary on the list. This example points out the broad salary range for people with MCSE certification, as well as how experience plays into salary offerings.

When you're searching for job opportunities after earning your MCSE certification, look beyond the classified ads in your local newspaper. If you only rely on newspapers for jobs, you're missing about 75 percent of what's available. Be sure to read Chapter 15, which lists ten Web sites for posting your resumé. These sites also offer you the chance to search for openings. In today's world, newspapers are a limited resource for finding the MCSE job that's right for you.

You also want to check out the various trade magazines that address topics of interest to MCSEs, including *MCP Magazine*, *Windows NT Magazine*, and *Network*.

Is the MCSE Certification Right for You?

You *must* ask this question: Is the MCSE certification right for me? Obviously, no one can answer it for you. But many prospective MCSE candidates ask everyone but themselves about this important decision.

To help you decide whether MCSE certification is right for you, Microsoft offers an online seminar called "How to Become a Microsoft Certified Professional" at the following address:

```
www.microsoft.com/seminar/98/GSMC-English/portal.htm
```

This short program offers some hints from Microsoft's perspective about how to begin the certification process.

If you're a numbers person, and you need the figures to help you sort out your career choices, here are some excellent sources:

- ✔ *The Dictionary of Occupational Titles,* U.S. Government Printing Office. You can access this publication online at the following address:

   `www.wave.net/upg/immigrations/dot_index.html`

- ✔ *The Occupational Outlook Handbook,* Rosen Publishing Group. This handbook is available online at

   `stats.bls.gov/ocohome.htm`

Remember that these books are about all careers. But you can use them to check the status of the MCSE professional outlook.

Are you a computer industry newcomer?

You can become an MCSE without industry experience, but at some point, hands-on practice and real-world networking knowledge become invaluable to your professional growth. Keep this idea in mind as you plan your MCSE certification path. Attempting to "dive-bomb" into the thick of it without a good foundation of the essentials will leave you, well, drowning.

When you become an MCSE, you will be expected to

- ✔ Know the answer to every question.
- ✔ Fix every problem.
- ✔ Be available at any time of the day or night.

Okay, maybe a little exaggeration — but not much. Just ask any of the professionals who already work in the industry!

Lots of people believe that anyone who has ever studied anything about a computer automatically knows the answer to every computer question. After you become certified, you'll be expected to know even more.

If you're new to the computer industry, you may find that your weakest area is understanding the hardware aspects of networking. In the next section of this chapter, we explain why hardware experience is so important.

How much hardware experience do you need?

As you work toward your MCSE certification, acquire as much knowledge as possible about computer and network hardware, including the types of wiring, network configurations, hubs, and routers. Somehow, some way, find a network on which you can experiment. Either build a network at home, find a job as an apprentice, volunteer to work for a company to gain experience, befriend a mentor, or stay after school and help the teacher.

You must pass a Networking Essentials exam to earn the MCSE certification. If you're new to the industry or if you've been a programmer, you may not have the hardware experience that's necessary for passing this test. If you need hardware experience, look for an ATEC (Authorized Technical Education Center) that offers a class in hardware.

In addition to aiming for the MCSE, you may want to consider pursuing the A+ certification. A+ certifies you to troubleshoot and repair computer hardware problems. Check out *A+ Certification For Dummies* for the full scope of A+ program information and testing requirements. Although A+ is not a Microsoft program, some ATECS may offer classes for A+ certification.

CompTIA (the Computer Technology Industry Association) creates the A+ certification exams, each of which averages from 75 to 100 questions and takes about $2^{1}/_{2}$ hours to complete. To earn A+ certification, you must pass two exams: a core exam, which crosses vendor platforms, and a Windows/DOS-specific exam.

Sylvan Prometric administers the A+ certification exams. For more information and the locations of testing centers, call 800-776-4276.

The Novell CNE (Certified Novell Engineer) programs also offer a hardware course that can help prepare you for the Networking Essentials exam. The class is called Networking Technologies. You have to pay separately to take the course because it isn't part of the MCSE certification track. Contact an ATEC that offers CNE programs for information.

What do I need to know about NetWare and UNIX?

You may be saying, "NetWare? UNIX? Are they still around?" First of all, we must warn you: Don't ask those questions of a CNE or a UNIX administrator. If you do, after picking yourself up off the floor, you'll realize that there is life after Microsoft. In fact, NetWare and UNIX were around before Windows NT networking products! And both of these platforms are used quite a bit in the marketplace.

Gaining experience on any NetWare or UNIX products can benefit you. In fact, many people achieve both the CNE and the MCSE certifications. This combination looks great to an employer.

If you can afford it, do both. The Novell classes and materials are structured so that the tests don't stray beyond the material that the textbooks cover. This focus makes the process of studying much easier than preparing for the MCSE certification, where exam questions often go outside the scope of Microsoft's official curriculum. (Another good reason to have the *Certification ...For Dummies* series. The books in this series tell you exactly what you need to know — and what you don't need to know — for the MCSE certification exams.) The CNE exams, however, are as difficult as MCSE certification exams — at least that's what we're told.

A really good plan is to earn your MCSE certification and then request that an employer pay for your CNE training. Or, if you're a CNE, how about asking your employer to pay for your MCSE certification? Never hurts to ask — after all, you know you're worth it!

Why bother with certification?

Well, maybe you do know everything that's required for earning MCSE certification, but you're not enthused about having to prove your worth. Before you cross the certification process off your "things to think about today" list, you may want to consider two key questions:

- ✔ Is your salary where it should be?
- ✔ Would it be higher if you were certified?

If you're already working as a network engineer and you're considering the MCSE certification simply as a formality, the benefits of certification depend on your employer.

Specifically, many employers offer bonuses and higher salaries to employees who earn MCSE certifications. And many employers pay employees' education and testing expenses; taking advantage of an employer's generosity makes sense.

What Does the MCSE Certification Require of You?

Surprising as it may seem, commitment is a primary requirement for earning MCSE certification — but not the only essential element. Actually, you need at least four important items:

✔ **Commitment.** Make a pact with yourself to "stay the course." We also suggest a reward system, which makes commitments easier and a lot more fun. For instance, promise to study three nights for two to three hours a night and reward yourself with a movie on the fourth night. After you pass a practice exam, think of another reward, only make it a little better. When you pass a real exam, treat yourself to dinner at your favorite restaurant. And when you finally earn your MCSE certification, take that vacation you've always wanted.

✔ **Time.** You can't make a commitment if you don't have the time. If the MCSE certification is what you want and you have no free time, you need to reprioritize your schedule to allow time for studying.

✔ **An open mind.** You need an open mind to understand the concepts and principles of networking, which often challenge traditional thinking.

✔ **A way to pay.** Because this is a book about the real world, we're telling you up front that securing the financial resources to accomplish your goals is a vital part of the whole process.

Avoiding excessive commitments

Just as you need to make a commitment to stick with the studies, you also need to eliminate clutter in your personal life so that you can fulfill your pledge to prepare for and pass the certification exams. By "clutter," we mean the social obligations that eat away at your calendar, leaving you feeling as though you never have enough hours in the day.

A fact of life: If you want to become an MCSE, you must make the time to study. We cover the process of developing your MCSE study plan in Chapter 4.

If you wait around for your MCSE certification without putting in the hard work, you can expect certification to always elude you. It's that simple. There's no such thing as MCSE-by-osmosis. For the next six months, plan to go straight home after work and study. You may have to cut down on your gym time while you're studying. The weekends at the beach may also have to go. (Although you can still reach your goals if you choose to take a book to the beach and study once in awhile.)

People who bring home paychecks learn that after the necessary deductions are made, they have to live with what's left over. The same principle applies as you try to figure out how to make the best use of the hours in your day. As they say, time is money — and MCSE certification study is a wise investment.

Balancing education with home and work

Finding time to concentrate on your MCSE certification studies while rearing a family may be the ultimate test. Obviously, you can't decide to stop caring for your children. However, just as finding time for your studies poses many possibilities, finding ways to fulfill your family responsibilities also provides an opportunity for creativity.

If you're married, maybe your spouse can take on a larger share of the household tasks on nights when you need to devote extra hours to studying. Just be sure that you return the favor by doing more than your share on other nights! And occasionally, at least once a week, get a baby-sitter so that both parents can take a break.

If you're a single parent, you have special challenges. Do you have relatives in town who can help you out? Perhaps a baby-sitter once in awhile? As a last resort, if nothing else works, wait for the children to be in bed before studying. Or, if you're too tired to study in the evening, try getting up an hour earlier every morning to hit the books. (Hey, if you can get up to jog, you can get up to study. Okay?)

As a favor to yourself, find a quiet place to study. A room with a door you can close is an absolute necessity. Don't have any? Then we seriously suggest that you go buy a door.

Nobody said preparing for MCSE certification exams would be easy, but every problem has a solution. Remember also that preparing for and obtaining your MCSE certification is a short-term challenge.

You Need the Right Tools

Before you begin any job, you need the right tools. Finding out about MCSE certification requires the same preparation.

In this section, we outline the tools and the preparatory work you need to do *before* you take any exams, even before you start to study.

Being an MCSE reporter

If you want to do this MCSE certification thing right, you need to take control of the process. To do so, you need to be just like a reporter, sniffing out a story. You need to learn all the facts. If you don't get the facts, you can't report the entire story, and then your readers won't get an accurate report.

To decide whether you should pursue MCSE certification, you must be both the reporter and the reader.

Do you want to make one of the more important decisions of your life armed with all the facts? Or are you satisfied to rely upon partial information?

Wouldn't you prefer to spend your time and money on something that you have verified as legitimate and worth the expense?

Starting your MCSE journal

A good reporter takes notes, so start a journal to record what you uncover. Then you have something to refer back to when you need to confirm or deny information.

As you investigate your MCSE options, you're also developing your MCSE reporting skills. If you see an advertisement in a magazine for an MCSE resource, don't just jot down the name, telephone number, and Web site address. Write down questions like these and include an answer that makes sense to you:

- How can they advertise a money-back guarantee?
- What are the conditions for reimbursement?
- What special features do they offer?
- Do they require payment for everything up front?

You may find that your answers prompt you to think of more questions. And this domino effect is *exactly* what should be happening in your fact-finding.

If you feel like you are not very good at asking questions, don't worry, you are not alone. Asking questions is a skill that you develop by practicing. You can determine your own approach by doing.

So jump right in and start practicing.

Guidelines for exploring the MCSE

First, remember to always keep your journal with you. You need to write down everything you uncover about the MCSE certification process. You can't possibly recall everything you read or that someone tells you.

Your goal is to explore everything. The only way that you can dig out all kinds of details is by doing lots of research, checking every source you can find. Ask lots of questions. Ask anyone and everyone.

Use the following ideas as guidelines for the questions you ask. If they seem familiar, that's because they're the questions every reporter is taught in beginning journalism classes. These questions are used for good reason; they cover the basics of good investigation.

Commit these questions to memory:

- ✔ Who?
- ✔ What?
- ✔ When?
- ✔ Where?
- ✔ Why?
- ✔ How?

And for your MCSE investigation, add the following two questions:

- ✔ Recommendations?
- ✔ How does *anything* I'm investigating apply to me?

As we show you in the next section of this chapter, you can apply these questions throughout your MCSE investigation. In the meantime, begin practicing. The next time you see an advertisement for an MCSE-related resource that seems too good to be true, pull out your journal, and write down answers to these questions. Just the simple process of pausing to analyze can help you.

Applying guidelines to researching

You may benefit from having an example for applying a technique, so here's a scenario to get you going:

Your only information about MCSE certification is from a friend who recently passed all the certification exams. Your friend is a networking professional, already working in data processing. Your friend's employer paid all the costs of certification. After passing the last exam in the MCSE certification process, your friend received a 10 percent bonus and a 30 percent raise.

You decide to investigate the MCSE certification process after your friend tells you that you should become an MCSE because the field is "wide-open."

Now, apply the questions:

- ✔ **Who?** Is your friend a credible source or just trying to be a good friend? This question is always a hard one to answer. On one hand, you have someone who seems to be interested in your future. Or is your friend just wrapped up in his or her current success and projecting it out to you?

  In the long run, you should carefully consider any decision based on a friendly recommendation. If you begin your pursuit of MCSE certification and dislike it, you may blame your friend for getting you into something you're not suited for. On the other hand, you may be successful, in which case, you'll thank your friend profusely for the recommendation.

- Who are the movers and shakers in the IT industry?
- Which companies have opportunities for people who have earned MCSE certification?

✔ **What?** What do I need to do to find out whether I'm suited for the MCSE?

- Do I have the personality traits? The skills?
- What is required to work as an MCSE?
- What do MCSEs do every day?
- What are the salaries?
- What's the downside to working as an MCSE?

✔ **When?** When do MCSEs work?

- Are different shifts available?
- Are frequent overtime or odd hours required or expected?
- Is this a daytime-only, eight-hours-a-day job?

✔ **Where?** Where do I find more information?

- Who can I ask besides my friend?
- Where can MCSEs work besides systems administration?

✔ **Why?** Why do I want to pursue MCSE certification?

- Do I want to leave my current job?
- Am I suited for the MCSE?

✔ **How?** How do I manage the studying?

- Do I need to quit my job and study full-time?
- Can I do the studying while working?

And don't forget these other two questions:

✔ Recommendations?

✔ How does *anything* I'm investigating apply to me?

Remember, this example can help you get rolling with your questions. Now, think of additional questions you can ask and keep a record of these questions in your journal.

Applying guidelines to interviews

During the process of deciding how, and whether, to become certified, you need to do interviews, including prospective employers, colleagues, and other MCSEs in the field. Again, here are some basic guidelines for the questions you can ask:

- ✔ **Who?** When you ask someone "who?" you want to know their credentials and experience.

- ✔ **What?** What is the working environment like?

  - What is a *typical* day like?

  - What don't you like about being an MCSE?

  - What kind of training did you have to become an MCSE?

  - What do you recommend for me?

  - What is your career path? Future plans?

  - What are typical salaries?

  - What are the negative aspects of the MCSE?

- ✔ **When?** What hours do you work?

  - Are you ever on call?

  - Do you carry a pager?

  - Are there sacrifices I can expect to make if I'm an MCSE?

  - When did you study for your MCSE exams? At night? Full-time during the day?

- ✔ **Where?** Where do you work?

  - Who do you work with?

  - Do you have an office?

  - Do you interact with lots of people in your daily routine?

  - Where did you get your professional training?

- ✔ **Why?** Why did you become an MCSE?

  - Why should I become an MCSE?

- ✔ **How?** How do you like being an MCSE?

  - Were you in the computer industry before becoming an MCSE? If not, what field?

  - If yes, did you have lots of hardware or software experience?

  - How would you advise me to cope with a lack of hardware experience?

- ✔ Recommendations?

- ✔ How does *anything* I'm investigating apply to me?

Always ask this question: "If you could tell me only one thing about becoming an MCSE, what would that be?"

Chapter 2

Weighing Your Certification Options

● ●

In This Chapter

▶ Understanding the benefits of certification

▶ Becoming a Microsoft Certified Professional, or MCP

▶ Earning certification as a Microsoft Certified Systems Engineer, or MCSE

▶ Examining the other Microsoft certifications

● ●

*A*lthough you may hear the most about the MCSE certification, Microsoft offers other certification options. Even within the MCSE, you can choose various areas of specialization that include responsibilities beyond those that most people associate with the MCSE. So while you may begin as a systems administrator, you may later choose to focus your skills as a TCP/IP specialist, or broaden your skills to include Internet network management. This chapter explores those choices and the benefits you can expect from certification.

Considering the Benefits of Certification

All the Microsoft certifications carry a lot of weight in the computer industry. In addition to receiving a nice certificate (suitable for framing) and a few other perks, you have the prestige of putting the professional designation of MCP, MCSE, MCSD, or MCT after your name. These benefits, plus the respect of your peers, puts you in an enviable position.

Here are some of the other benefits that you receive with the certifications. Keep in mind that the higher your level of certification, the greater your benefits.

✔ **Online forums.** You can access several dedicated MCP forums on the Microsoft Network (MSN).

✔ **MCP Magazine.** After passing your first MCP exam, you receive a free, one-year subscription to *MCP Magazine*. This publication includes articles about specific certification exams, readers' experiences as MCPs, and updates on certifications.

✔ **Newsletter.** Microsoft automatically sends an MCP newsletter to any MCP with an e-mail account. If you don't get yours, you can subscribe by going to the MCP Web site, at `www.microsoft.com/mcp` or `register.microsoft.com/regwiz/personalinfo.asp`.

✔ **Microsoft Web sites.** Microsoft has MCP, MCSE, MCSD, and MCT private Web sites. To access each of these sites, you must have the corresponding certification level. Each Web site has different levels of additional benefits.

✔ **Logos.** After achieving each certification, you receive a packet of logos representing that particular program. Following guidelines that accompany the packet, you can use the logos on your business cards, stationery, and other Microsoft-approved materials.

✔ **TechNet.** As an MCSE, you receive a free, one-year subscription to TechNet. TechNet, provided by Microsoft, is a technical resource with no equal. Your monthly CD includes nearly every bit of technical advice Microsoft has available about its products.

✔ **Beta software program.** As an MCSE, you receive a one-year, once-in-a-lifetime subscription to the monthly beta software-mailing program.

✔ **Events.** After you're certified, you can attend and participate in all kinds of Microsoft conventions and meetings. You'll receive e-mail messages inviting you to a variety of conferences and training events. You also can find out what's going on by visiting the following Web site:

```
www.microsoft.com/events/
```

Understanding the MCP and MCSE Certifications

Okay, here goes. Knowing the differences between the certifications can be a little tricky at first. You're likely to hear enough abbreviations to turn your brain into alphabet soup. Nevertheless, you can make sense of this stuff if you read through this chapter.

Just remember that the MCP is the starting point.

The Microsoft Certified Professional — MCP

As a first goal, plan to become an MCP, or Microsoft Certified Professional. The MCP certification is the foundation — the place where all Microsoft certifications begin.

Earning MCP certification has several benefits:

- ✔ You find out what Microsoft's certification exams are like, and passing your first exam bolsters your confidence for the next one.
- ✔ You can list the MCP title after your name on your resumé or other promotional materials.
- ✔ You gain access to the private MCP Web site, www.microsoft.com/mcp.
- ✔ You receive an MCP certificate, suitable for framing.
- ✔ You receive a free, one-year subscription to *MCP Magazine*.
- ✔ You get MCP logos suitable for use on your business cards and stationery.
- ✔ Most importantly, prospective employers know that you have passed an exam, certifying your expertise with an operating system or key Microsoft technologies.

The MCP program changed in the fall of 1998. Before then, you had to be certified in a Microsoft operating system. But the rules have changed. In the following sections, we explain the old and new ways for earning the MCP certification.

The way it was

Before fall 1998, Microsoft Certified Professional candidates were required to pass a Microsoft exam based on a Windows server or desktop operating system. *Note:* Not all MCP exams contribute to an MCSE certificate. In fact, not very many do! Be sure to check the official Microsoft requirements when you make your MCSE plans. Although we do our best to make this book as up-to-date as possible, everything changes — especially Microsoft stuff.

The new MCP plan

As of October 1, 1998, you can become an MCP by passing *any* certification exam, with the following exceptions:

- ✔ Networking Essentials
- ✔ Any retired exams

Take your first exam as soon as you're ready. After you pass that first qualifying exam, your official registration as an MCP takes anywhere from two to four weeks. You'll receive a welcome packet in the mail, signaling that the registration is complete and your MCP benefits then begin.

Everyone has different goals. If you want to become an MCP, select those exams that correspond to your needs. For instance, if you're interested in the MCSE+Internet certification because of the Internet connection, know that Microsoft also offers an MCP+Internet certification. Check out the MCP Web site at www.microsoft.com/mcp to see the latest available choices.

Regardless of which path you choose, you should still prepare for and take the Networking Essentials exam. Take this exam even if you don't plan to become an MCSE. Understanding networking hardware can help you trouble-shoot a lot of difficult situations.

The Microsoft Certified Systems Engineer — MCSE

The explosive growth of computer networks has created a huge demand for professionals to manage them. The job of the person holding the MCSE certification is to manage those networks using Microsoft products, specifically Windows NT software. Gaining MCSE certification brings industry recognition, as well as the promise of a very exciting, busy, and demanding career.

Taking a look at the MCSE exam requirements

To earn MCSE certification, you must pass six exams:

- ✔ Four core exams: Networking Essentials and three exams that test operating system proficiency. The core exam choices for operating systems are Windows NT Workstation, Windows NT Server, Windows NT Server in the Enterprise, Windows 95, and Windows 98.

- ✔ Two electives, offering you an opportunity to specialize. Elective choices include TCP/IP, MS Exchange, SQL Server, Proxy Server, and SNA Server.

We detail your choices for the core and elective exams in Chapter 3.

When you investigate the MCSE exams, ignore any mention of the 3.51 track. Microsoft plans to retire the 3.51 exams when the next release of Windows NT debuts in 1999. Focus your attention on becoming certified in either Windows NT 4.0 or the new release, when it's available.

How long will it take to get my MCSE?

Time limits don't apply to the MCSE certification process. In fact, you can take as long as you want.

Be realistic with your goals, however. Stringing the process out indefinitely, without goal-setting, accomplishes nothing. In fact, you'll probably tire of the whole prolonged business and quit.

So what's the verdict? Well, if you're ambitious, have the time and the self-discipline, you can become certified in six months. On the other hand, you may need a year or more, if your circumstances constrain you.

Two years? Three years? Try to avoid dragging out the certification process to such lengths. Make a rigorous plan — one that's challenging yet not discouraging — and stick to it. In Chapter 4, we explain how to develop a schedule for your studying and exams.

Retired exams don't count toward your MCSE certification. If you pass an exam and then Microsoft retires it before you become an MCSE, you must take a replacement exam within six months. You can always find out which exams are current by going to www.microsoft.com/mcp and choosing a certification program link.

Checking Out Other Microsoft Certifications

In the following sections, we tell you about three additional certifications that may interest you. Okay, we know this book is about the MCSE, but you need to know the options — at least the major ones.

Don't limit yourself to investigating just the MCSE. Remember to keep an open mind when you're thinking about your career! And don't forget to check the MCP Web site at www.microsoft.com/mcp for updates and new programs.

For more information about training and certification for Microsoft products and technologies, visit the Microsoft Training and Certification Web site at www.Microsoft.com/Train_Cert/. This site offers information about Microsoft certification programs, and it identifies resources available to help you get trained and certified.

The MCSE+Internet

The MCSE+Internet is the MCSE program with additional exams that test your ability to work with the Internet and intranet sites, both of which are hot topics right now. With the growth of e-commerce, or electronic commerce, you may want to consider adding the Internet option to your MCSE certification.

Chapter 3 lists the exams that you need for the MCSE+Internet certification. And the other books in the *Certification …For Dummies* series tell you what you need to know to pass these exams.

You can find more information about the MCSE+Internet certification at www.microsoft.com/mcp/mktg/mcsei.htm.

The Microsoft Certified Solutions Developer — MCSD

Unlike the MCSE, who administers the network, a Microsoft Certified Solutions Developer (MCSD) designs solutions to network and information systems problems. An MCSD who works with Windows NT Server focuses primarily on BackOffice products, including such offerings as SQL Server, Visual Basic, and Microsoft Access.

Here are some of the real-world duties of an MCSD:

- ✔ Working on teams designing software and databases
- ✔ Analyzing problems and designing systems solutions
- ✔ Testing and debugging software
- ✔ Suggesting hardware and software upgrades
- ✔ Developing software documentation

For more details about becoming an MCSD, see the Microsoft Web page at

www.microsoft.com/mcp/certstep/mcsd.htm

As with the MCP program, Microsoft changed the certification requirements for the MCSD in the fall of 1998. Checking the Web site for changes is always a good idea.

Rumor has it that Microsoft is developing an MCSD+Internet certification. Check the MCSD Web site for current information.

The Microsoft Certified Trainer — MCT

The MCT, or Microsoft Certified Trainer, certification is for those people who want to teach MCP curriculum at ATECs (Authorized Technical Education Centers), AATPs (Authorized Academic Training Partners), or wherever. If you don't plan to teach at an ATEC, the MCT certification lends extra credibility to your level of expertise in an office environment or other training setting.

If you plan to teach at an ATEC, you must be certified in the instruction that you want to provide.

If you want to pursue the MCT certification, visit the MCT Web site to review the guidelines:

```
www.microsoft.com/mcp/certstep/mct.htm
```

To earn MCT certification, you must attend the required Microsoft trainer course, Train-the-Trainer, or prove that you possess the skills to train according to the MCT guidelines.

At the Web site, you can also print out the MCT application. After earning your required training certification, you can submit the MCT application, along with your MCP/MCSE transcripts, certificate of attendance from one Microsoft course you've attended, and the *Preparation to Teach* checklist (part of the MCT guidelines).

The fee to become an MCT is $200 for freelance trainers, or free if you're associated with an ATEC or AATP.

Of course, Microsoft is constantly tinkering with the MCT program. Make sure that you visit the Web site to stay in tune with current guidelines.

Chapter 3
Getting on the Right MCSE Track

• •

In This Chapter

▶ Finding out about the MCSE core exams

▶ Understanding your choices among the MCSE elective exams

▶ Checking out requirements for MCSE+Internet certification

▶ Using the Microsoft exam preparation guides

▶ Identifying retired exams

• •

The MCSE is only one of several Microsoft certifications that you may choose to pursue. (See Chapter 2 for descriptions of other certifications that Microsoft offers.) And even after you decide that you want to earn MCSE certification, you have still more choices to make. First, you need to determine which core exams you plan to take. The decision-making's pretty straightforward, because your choices are limited.

Next, you need to pick the elective exams that you want to take to complete your certification. This decision is a little trickier, because you have more choices. You can compare this process to choosing a major in high school or college. You can always change your mind, but you're better off knowing what you want in advance.

In this chapter, we describe your choices for core and elective MCSE certification exams. We also list the requirements for the MCP and MCSE+Internet certifications. We show you where to find helpful exam preparation information on the Microsoft Web site, and we explain how to find out about retired exams.

To help you figure out which certification track you want to follow, Microsoft offers an online aptitude test at the following address:

```
partnering3.microsoft.com/skills2000/default.asp
```

Sorting Out Your Exam Choices

As we mention in Chapter 2, Microsoft offers several certifications in addition to the MCSE. We focus on the MCSE certification throughout this book, but we also want to fill you in on some other certification options.

When viewed as the first step toward becoming an MCSE, the MCP designation shows that you have in-depth knowledge of at least one Microsoft operating system. You become an MCP by passing *any* certification exam, with the exception of Networking Essentials. And of course, retired exams don't count for MCP certification.

To earn MCSE or MCSE+Internet certification, you must pass a specified number of exams. Table 3-1 lists the general requirements for these certifications.

Table 3-1	How Many Exams Does It Take?	
	MCSE	*MCSE+Internet*
Core Exams	4	7
Elective Exams	2	3

You can take the exams in any order you choose. However, we suggest that you complete the core requirements first. For the elective exams, such as TCP/IP, Internet Information Server, and Exchange, you must have a solid knowledge of the Windows NT operating system.

Cutting to the core

You have some latitude even within the core requirements for the MCSE and MCSE+Internet certifications. For example, the requirements for MCSE certification include earning credit for four core exams. Microsoft specifies three of those exams, but you have several choices for the fourth core exam. Similarly, you have various choices for the seven core exams that you must pass to earn MCSE+Internet certification.

Core exams for the MCSE certification

To achieve the MCSE certification, you must earn credit for the following core exams:

- Exam 70-067, Implementing and Supporting Microsoft Windows NT Server 4.0
- Exam 70-068, Implementing and Supporting Microsoft Windows NT Server 4.0 in the Enterprise
- Exam 70-058, Networking Essentials

You must also pass a fourth core exam and two electives. You can choose any one of the following exams as the fourth core exam:

- ✔ Exam 70-064, Implementing and Supporting Microsoft Windows 95
- ✔ Exam 70-073, Implementing and Supporting Microsoft Windows NT Workstation 4.0
- ✔ Exam 70-098, Implementing and Supporting Microsoft Windows 98

The section "Choosing your elective exams," later in this chapter, lists your choices for the two elective exams that you need to pass to complete the requirements for your MCSE certification.

You can earn credit for Networking Essentials — one of the core requirements for the MCSE and MCSE+Internet certifications — if you supply proof of certification in a Novell, Banyan, or Sun network operating environment. The relevant Novell certifications are

- ✔ **CNE** — Certified Novell Engineer
- ✔ **CNI** — Certified Novell Instructor
- ✔ **ECNE** — Enterprise Certified Novell Engineer
- ✔ **MCNE** — Master Certified Novell Engineer

For Banyan, the certifications are

- ✔ **CBE** — Certified Banyan Engineer
- ✔ **CBS** — Certified Banyan Specialist

And here are your choices for Sun certifications:

- ✔ **CNA** — Sun Certified Network Administrator for Solaris 2.5
- ✔ **CNA** — Sun Certified Network Administrator for Solaris 2.6

Core exams for MCSE+Internet

To complete the core requirements for the MCSE+Internet certification, you must earn credit for seven core exams:

- ✔ Exam 70-058, Networking Essentials
- ✔ Exam 70-059, Internetworking Microsoft TCP/IP on Microsoft Windows NT 4.0

- ✔ Exam 70-064, Implementing and Supporting Microsoft Windows 95, or Exam 70-073, Implementing and Supporting Microsoft Windows NT Workstation 4.0, or Exam 70-098, Implementing and Supporting Microsoft Windows 98

  Note: Microsoft accepts certification in retired Exam 70-063, Implementing and Supporting Microsoft Windows 95 as an alternative to Exam 70-064.

- ✔ Exam 70-067, Implementing and Supporting Microsoft Windows NT Server 4.0

- ✔ Exam 70-068, Implementing and Supporting Microsoft Windows NT Server 4.0 in the Enterprise

- ✔ Exam 70-077, Implementing and Supporting Microsoft Internet Information Server 3.0 and Microsoft Index Server 1.1, or Exam 70-087, Implementing and Supporting Microsoft Internet Information Server 4.0

- ✔ Exam 70-079, Implementing and Supporting Microsoft Internet Explorer 4.0 by using the Internet Explorer Administration Kit

In addition to the seven core exams, you must pass three elective exams to earn your MCSE+Internet certification. (See "Choosing your elective exams," later in this chapter.)

If you already have professional certification in a Novell, Banyan, or Sun networking environment, you may be able to get credit for Exam 70-058, Networking Essentials, without taking that core exam. For all the details, see the section "Core exams for the MCSE certification," earlier in this chapter.

Which core exams are the hardest?

At some point, you may find yourself discussing the Microsoft certification exams with other IT professionals. Invariably, someone will bring up a tough exam experience. Someone else will chime in with a different opinion, and soon you'll be debating which exam is the hardest.

Oddly, no one seems to agree. Some people swear that the NT Server 4.0 exam is awful, while others dread NT Server 4.0 in the Enterprise. Still others believe that the first exam is the toughest, regardless of the subject.

The point is that each exam is tough for some people and relatively easy for others. You'll undoubtedly have similar war stories after you complete the MCSE certification process.

Use your best judgment

Ignore suggestions that a particular exam is a breeze. If you take such statements to heart, you may short-change your exam preparation. And if you aren't ready, you may fail the exam.

Go ahead and engage in a little water-cooler gossip if you're so inclined, but don't take anything you hear too seriously. If someone says the Enterprise exam is easy, smile and then go hit the books with extra fervor.

Personally, we think all the exams are hard.

Do I have to take the exams in a certain order?

Microsoft doesn't specify a required sequence for taking the exams. And if you ask two MCSEs to recommend the order in which you should take the core exams, you can expect two different answers. Ask ten MCSEs and . . . Well, you get the idea.

The most frequently suggested order is

- ✔ First: Exam 70-058, Networking Essentials
- ✔ Then: Exam 70-073, Implementing and Supporting Microsoft Windows NT Workstation 4.0
- ✔ Next: Exam 70-067, Implementing and Supporting Microsoft Windows NT Server 4.0
- ✔ And finally: Exam 70-068, Implementing and Supporting Microsoft Windows NT Server 4.0 in the Enterprise

Although Microsoft doesn't require a particular exam order, the exams do tend to build upon each other. For example, the exams on Windows NT Workstation and NT Server assume that you have mastered Networking Essentials, and the NT Server in the Enterprise exam assumes that you have mastered the Workstation and Server exams. Likewise, the electives assume that you have mastered the core requirements.

Choosing your elective exams

The core requirements for the MCSE+Internet certification include a few options, but you really don't have much room to maneuver when you're looking at the core exams for the MCSE. On the other hand, you have lots of choices among the elective exams.

MCSE electives

In addition to earning credit for four core exams (see "Cutting to the core," earlier in this chapter), you must pass two elective exams to earn MCSE certification. You have the following choices for MCSE elective exams:

✔ Exam 70-013, Implementing and Supporting Microsoft SNA Server 3.0, or Exam 70-085, Implementing and Supporting Microsoft SNA Server 4.0

✔ Exam 70-018, Implementing and Supporting Microsoft Systems Management Server 1.2, or Exam 70-086, Implementing and Supporting Microsoft Systems Management Server 2.0

✔ Exam 70-021, Microsoft SQL Server 4.2 Database Implementation, or Exam 70-027, Implementing a Database Design on Microsoft SQL Server 6.5, or Exam 70-029, Designing and Implementing Databases with Microsoft SQL Server 7.0

Note: Microsoft has announced plans to retire Exam 70-021, Microsoft SQL Server 4.2 Database Implementation.

✔ Exam 70-022, Microsoft SQL Server 4.2 Database Administration for Microsoft Windows NT, or Exam 70-026, System Administration for Microsoft SQL Server 6.5, or Exam 70-028, Administering Microsoft SQL Server 7.0

Note: Microsoft recently released plans to retire Exam 70-022, Microsoft SQL Server 4.2 Database Administration for Microsoft Windows NT.

✔ Exam 70-037, Microsoft Mail for PC Networks 3.2 - Enterprise

Note: Microsoft plans to retire this exam.

✔ Exam 70-053, Internetworking Microsoft TCP/IP on Microsoft Windows NT (3.5–3.51), or Exam 70-059, Internetworking with Microsoft TCP/IP on Microsoft Windows NT 4.0

✔ Exam 70-056, Implementing and Supporting Web Sites Using Microsoft Site Server 3.0

✔ Exam 70-076, Implementing and Supporting Microsoft Exchange Server 5, or Exam 70-081, Implementing and Supporting Microsoft Exchange Server 5.5

✔ Exam 70-077, Implementing and Supporting Microsoft Internet Information Server 3.0 and Microsoft Index Server 1.1, or Exam 70-087, Implementing and Supporting Microsoft Internet Information Server 4.0

✔ Exam 70-078, Implementing and Supporting Microsoft Proxy Server 1.0, or Exam 70-088, Implementing and Supporting Microsoft Proxy Server 2.0

✔ Exam 70-079, Implementing and Supporting Microsoft Internet Explorer 4.0 by Using the Internet Explorer Administration Kit

Several entries in the preceding list mention more than one exam. If you pass more than one exam from any of those groups, only one exam qualifies as an MCSE elective. You must pass one other exam to fulfill the requirement for two elective exams.

MCSE+Internet electives

You must pass seven core exams to earn MCSE+Internet certification. (For details, see the section "Cutting to the core," earlier in this chapter.) To complete your MCSE+Internet certification, you must also pass two elective exams. You have the following choices for MCSE+Internet electives:

- ✔ Exam 70-026, Administering Microsoft SQL Server 6.5, or Exam 70-028, Administering Microsoft SQL Server 7.0

- ✔ Exam 70-027, Implementing a Database Design on Microsoft SQL Server 6.5, or Exam 70-029, Designing and Implementing Databases with Microsoft SQL Server 7.0

- ✔ Exam 70-056, Implementing and Supporting Web Sites Using Microsoft Site Server 3.0

- ✔ Exam 70-076, Implementing and Supporting Microsoft Exchange Server 5, or Exam 70-081, Implementing and Supporting Microsoft Exchange Server 5.5

- ✔ Exam 70-078, Implementing and Supporting Microsoft Proxy Server 1.0, or Exam 70-088, Implementing and Supporting Microsoft Proxy Server 2.0

- ✔ Exam 70-085, Implementing and Supporting Microsoft SNA Server 4.0

Which electives are the hardest?

As we mention earlier in this chapter (see the section "Which core exams are the hardest?"), everyone has an opinion about the difficulty (or ease) of passing the various certification exams. We think the exams are all challenging, but we also believe that a few electives deserve special attention during your preparation for the certification exams:

- ✔ **SQL Server:** Some MCSE candidates find databases intimidating. Be prepared to spend extra time preparing for these exams.

- ✔ **TCP/IP:** TCP/IP gives many people headaches because of the sections on subnetting and binary math. Be sure to work lots of sample problems when you're preparing for this exam.

- ✔ **Exchange Server:** This exam involves lots of terminology and concepts that may be unfamiliar to you.

When You're Down to the Last Exam and You Just Want to Get It Over With

As you approach the end of the certification process, we have a good idea how you'll answer the following questions:

- ✔ Are you so sick of this stuff that you can't stand it?
- ✔ Do you want to study something fun for a change?
- ✔ Do you just want to get your certification?

Unfortunately, you won't come across any really easy exams during the MCSE certification process. If you need a change of pace, however, consider taking Exam 70-079, Implementing and Supporting Microsoft Internet Explorer 4.0 by Using the Internet Explorer Administration Kit (IEAK).

You have to study and prepare for this exam as much as you do for all the other exams. However, we think you may enjoy learning about the IEAK, which enables systems administrators to customize IE in a LAN environment by using scripts.

Examining the Exam Preparation Guides

As you prepare for each exam, you need to pattern your studies after the exam objectives that Microsoft lists in its respective exam preparation guide. Each exam preparation guide lists the skills you must master to pass a particular exam. (For even more details about the exam preparation guides, refer to Chapter 4.)

Appendix D lists the objectives for each of the MCSE core exams.

To find the exam preparation guides online:

1. **Go to the Microsoft Training and Certification Web site, at the following address:**

```
www.microsoft.com/train_cert/
```

2. **Click the** Find an Exam **link.**

3. **On the search page that's displayed, use the drop-down lists to select the product and the certification that you want.**

   You see a list of available certification exams for the specified product.

4. **Click the link for the exam that you want.**

   Your browser displays the exam preparation guide for the selected exam.

Each exam preparation guide includes a section titled "Skills Being Measured." This section of an exam preparation guide lists the job skills, or exam subjects, that you need to know. Although the Skills Being Measured differ for each exam, Microsoft uses six categories to organize the objectives for each exam:

✔ Planning

✔ Installation and Configuration

✔ Managing Resources

✔ Connectivity

✔ Monitoring and Optimization

✔ Troubleshooting

Everything about a Microsoft certification exam — including preparation, exam questions, and exam results — revolves around these six categories. When you finish an exam, for example, you see the results, both on screen and in hard copy, listed in these six categories. This information is very helpful for pinpointing areas of weakness.

Finding Out about Retired Exams

Occasionally, Microsoft retires an exam. We do everything we can to ensure that this book contains the latest information, but you can get even more up-to-date information about retired exams by visiting the following Web page:

```
www.microsoft.com/train_cert/mcp/examinfo/retired.htm
```

Retired exams don't count toward your certification. So if you're halfway to your certification and Microsoft retires an exam you've taken, you need to take the exam that replaces the retired exam, or one that qualifies for credit toward your certification.

Part II

The Journey Begins — Studying for Your MCSE

The 5th Wave   By Rich Tennant

"We sort of have our own way of mentally preparing our people to take an MCSE exam."

In this part . . .

*B*eing productive while studying for your MCSE exams and enjoying the enriching experience are not always birds of a feather. You can probably think of a million other things you'd rather be doing than organizing your study plans and hitting the books.

Yet you do want the MCSE certification, right? So why not take the time to do it effectively so that you can move past test-taking and start applying yourself in a great job?

In this part, you develop a plan to tackle your MCSE studies — right up to the moment when you face the real music. At the risk of sounding like a broken record, we emphasize the importance of staying focused on Microsoft's exam preparation guides. We help you get ready to hit the books, and we offer some useful ideas for making the most of your review and pre-exam practice time.

Chapter 4

Developing Your Personal MCSE Study Plan

• •

• •

*I*n this chapter, we show you how to create a master plan for your MCSE studies and develop an MCSE time management system. We also explain how you can realign your studying skills, applying them to your preparation for the certification exams.

This chapter also offers some conceptual material about planning, self-discipline, time management, and setting priorities — the kind of information you need, even if it is theory. Above all else, dive into this stuff with a plan to have fun. We think that the more you look for gratification in this process, the more creative you can become as you use what you discover along the way.

Understanding the Value of an MCSE Study Plan

Although the need for a personally tailored study plan may seem obvious, many people fail to follow through on this crucial element of ensuring their MCSE certification success. As cliché as the analogy sounds, imagine traveling to an unfamiliar city without taking a map or calling ahead for directions. Or, think about buying a house without checking out mortgage interest rates before you seal the deal.

Although you can get to where you're going without a map, a clear-cut plan makes the trip a lot simpler — and the route to your destination considerably less fraught with roadblocks. We observe two general groups of people in the MCSE certification process:

- ✔ **Those who invest an interest — when they have time.** Most people we know with this philosophy are still working toward their MCSE certifications.

- ✔ **Planners**. Many of these people are already MCSEs.

Which group sounds more appealing to you? Better yet, which of the two types of workers would you want managing your networks?

Don't let the phrase *study habits* scare you. Study habits are nothing more than a way of doing something. For successful students, the mode of operation is not so much habit as second nature. Through practice, these successful students have discarded old, ineffective ways of working through their studies.

But even successful students need to rethink the way they approach the MCSE exams. The Microsoft certification exams are so different that a lack of proper preparation catches many people off guard. Remember that dreaded high school or college class you thought was difficult? It was a piece of cake compared to working on your MCSE certification. Of course, we don't want to frighten you away from following through the process, but many people fail to finish the MCSE because they assume that their old study habits and exam-taking methods can translate to certification success. The leap from tried and true to something new usually requires much bigger steps.

The Microsoft exams are so difficult for several reasons, including:

- ✔ **Terminology:** You have to learn more computer terms and acronyms than you even realized existed.

- ✔ **Details:** You may know everything about getting around the NT operating system — but that isn't enough. You have to learn and memorize what happens beneath the user interface.

- ✔ **Microsoft is not an island:** You may think otherwise — until you discover that the exams expect you to know a little about other systems, such as UNIX and NetWare.

- ✔ **Complex exam questions:** The questions are often difficult to read and decipher.

- ✔ **Time:** You have a time limit — usually 90 minutes. You must quickly find the answer among your multiple choices!

Whether you're confident with your study habits or you're well aware that your exam approach could use some polish, you need to consider some changes to tackle the MCSE exams. But don't worry, the techniques in this book can bring your study skills to full blossom. When you practice what you read here, you're on your way to certification success!

Prioritizing the important stuff

When you begin making your study plans for each exam and your overall MCSE track, you have to take a hard look at the responsibilities you already have. These obligations include your job, your family, and other daily or weekly responsibilities you may face. Looking at these factors can help you determine how much time each day you can devote to study and preparation.

You not only have to prioritize your study time, but you also have to prioritize *how* you plan to study the content. Exam success usually calls for memorizing the material, especially minor details. Those small details are easy to forget, even when you stay focused on knowing them by heart. For example, the Networking Essentials exam presents lots of terms and cable specifications that require memorization. You have to use the Microsoft exam preparation guides (which we explore in the section "Finding Out about This Thing Called an Exam Preparation Guide," later in this chapter) to prioritize the material you study, and then keep reviewing that material over and over — even after you can recite it in your sleep.

That's why prioritizing is vital to certification success. You must stay focused on what you are doing at that moment. Your studies must take priority over most other things you may want to do. Otherwise, you may as well go to the movies, because, quite frankly, you will absorb more about networking from the movie *Lethal Weapon* than you will from your *MCSE ...For Dummies* book if you don't have your priorities in the proper order.

With a little help from your friends

While having a study partner is always a helpful option, we want to take the pairing-up concept a bit further. Do you have a group of friends who want to earn MCSE certification? Then consider creating an MCSE study team. With a little planning, you can bring a group of people together, all of whom share a common goal.

You can share each other's war stories, help your fellow students in a bind, and even enjoy free time together as you work off the stress. Creating an MCSE study team is an exciting idea for getting through the grind of the certification process. The team approach is also an excellent way to exercise your planning skills. Your own MCSE study team can be two people or ten.

So if studying for your exams is your top priority, how can you maintain your priorities? One of the better things you can do is have a self-proclaimed place of study. It may be a room, a porch, the attic, the roof — whatever, but you must have a place where you can go to study and avoid distractions. You can't study in front of the television and you can't study with other people around. Find a place that works for you and helps you to keep your study priority in focus.

Why planning can empower your progress

Now, are you convinced that planning your MCSE studies is important? If you intend to earn MCSE certification, you need to demonstrate good planning skills. Don't underestimate this fact.

Look at the sample exam preparation guide in the section "Exploring an exam preparation guide," later in this chapter. *Planning* ranks on the top of the list, and it's also the first focal category on the exams. Doesn't that give you a pretty good idea of the importance of planning?

Developing your planning skills doesn't happen overnight. Moreover, if this first step is an area of deficiency, the best place and time to begin to mend those shortcomings is here and now. Plan your certification path and make it happen. Doing so can prove to yourself and others that you have what it takes to pass these exams, which is what employers are looking for — employees with the stamina to finish the exams. They know that these people can withstand the rigor of working with information systems.

Creating Study Schedules and Sticking to Them

- ✔ Be flexible.
- ✔ Be realistic.

Ignoring both of these platitudes creates stress that can limit your ability to perform at your peak. So how do you create a workable plan? The bottom line is really just common sense:

- Create a *realistic* plan.
- *Obey* your plan, becoming single-minded, or driven, in pursuit of your goals.
- Set *sensible* goals. In other words, don't overdo it.
- Give yourself a break occasionally. After all, you're only human.

We believe wholeheartedly that if you follow this advice, you can earn MCSE certification — after all, we've seen it happen.

In the same way that you give success your best shot, you can set yourself up for certain failure. And the easiest way to ensure failure is to commit yourself to more than you're capable of accomplishing. When outlining your study plan and the exam content, keep in mind that you have to constantly review what you already know. You can't read through a preparation book of any kind without constantly reviewing what you've learned in the previous chapters. Make sure that your plan allows ample time for review of content you've already covered. Ideally, you should devote the first one-third of your study to return to previously studied terms, procedures, and concepts.

Practice working within a well-defined schedule. Inexperienced planners create unrealistic schedules. Although the tasks we recommend may sound excessive and elementary, these tips can help you approach scheduling realistically.

So, for the time being, try the following steps to help you get in the habit of scheduling your whole day. Just humor us; we promise the results are worth it.

- Write *everything* down, at least in the beginning. Write down your work schedule, family commitments, chores, and errands — everything! Recognizing the full range of your time commitments can enable you to develop a realistic feel for a workable schedule.
- Review your plans every couple of hours. Even if you have no changes to make, just glance at your schedule. You can become more attuned to where your time really goes — and how to manage the flow.
- Don't let the schedule stress you out. Your daily schedule and your study schedule are supposed to help you stay on track toward completion. But life in general is difficult to schedule because so many things come up to interfere with your plans. The point is, adhere to the schedule as much as possible, but be flexible so that you can bend without breaking when you need to adjust.

Life does not like schedules

Face the facts: Inevitably, something happens to throw your study schedule off track. You just have to know how to recover in an effective manner. Say you're preparing for the Networking Essentials exam, and your schedule dictates that you study for three hours each evening. Now, imagine that one day you have to stay late at work and do not get home until 8 p.m. Keeping your study schedule at this point is not the wisest decision. Studying for awhile is okay, but you really need to realign your plans for the next several days. *Covering* the material is not enough; *knowing* the content is key to exam success.

If you want to survive the MCSE certification process, stay out of the Internet chat rooms. These places are time-killers. If you are a chat-room junkie, and you have to stop by sometimes, then set clear time limits and stick to the schedule.

Finding Out about This Thing Called an Exam Preparation Guide

In the preceding sections of this chapter, we talk about the importance of planning and prioritizing your schedule so that you can tackle your studies. The rest of this chapter takes a hands-on approach to assembling your study materials, organizing a schedule, and preparing to study for a certification exam. You begin this process with the Microsoft exam preparation guides.

We list the exam preparation guides for the core MCSE exams in Appendix D of this book. However, be forewarned that Microsoft's exam objectives change from time to time — and without notice — so it's always a good idea to check the Microsoft Web site to make sure that you have the most up-to-date exam preparation guides.

To access the latest copy of an exam preparation guide:

1. **Go to the MCP Web site** (www.microsoft.com/mcp)**, shown in Figure 4-1.**

2. **At the MCP Web site, click the** Find Exam **link in the left column.**

    As shown in Figure 4-2, you see a search page with drop-down lists for specifying the product and the certification that you want.

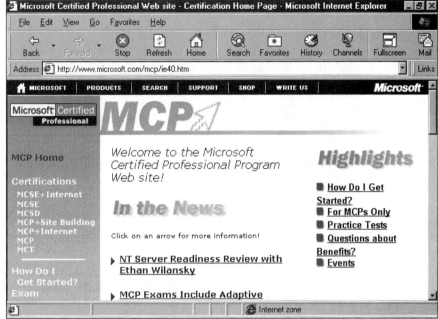

Figure 4-1:
Use the
MCP Web
site to find
exam
preparation
guides.

3. Select the desired product and certification, and then click Go.

You see a list of available exams for the selected product and certification.

4. Click the link for the exam you want.

Like Microsoft magic, the exam preparation guide appears, as shown in Figure 4-3.

Each exam preparation guide contains general information about the exam and official curriculum courses. The objectives for the exam are usually listed at the bottom of the screen.

Web watch

While pursuing your MCSE certification, try to get in the habit of checking www.microsoft.com/mcp on a regular basis. This way, you can keep track of any certification changes, exam changes, or new certification options coming your way from Microsoft.

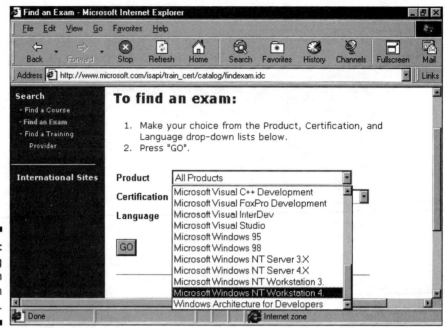

Figure 4-2:
Searching
for an exam
preparation
guide.

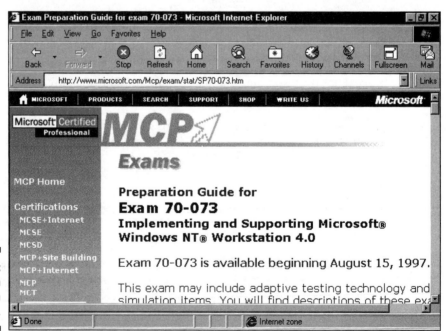

Figure 4-3:
The exam
preparation
guide.

Exploring an exam preparation guide

Now, the term *exam preparation guide* is rather misleading — actually, you end up with the objectives for each exam and not much else. The categories simply tell you what Microsoft expects you to know for the exam and what content is testable. To see what we mean, take a look at the exam preparation guide for Exam 70-073, Implementing and Supporting Microsoft Windows NT 4.0 Workstation:

Planning

✔ Create unattended installation files.

✔ Plan strategies for sharing and securing resources.

✔ Choose the appropriate file system to use in a given situation. File systems and situations include:

- NTFS

- FAT

- HPFS

- Security

- Dual-boot systems

Installation and Configuration

✔ Install Windows NT Workstation on an Intel platform in a given situation.

✔ Set up a dual-boot system in a given situation.

✔ Remove Windows NT Workstation in a given situation.

✔ Install, configure, and remove hardware components for a given situation. Hardware components include:

- Network adapter drivers

- SCSI device drivers

- Tape device drivers

- UPS

- Multimedia devices

- Display drivers

- Keyboard drivers

- Mouse drivers

- ✔ Use Control Panel applications to configure a Windows NT Workstation computer in a given situation.
- ✔ Upgrade to Windows NT Workstation 4.0 in a given situation.
- ✔ Configure server-based installation for wide-scale deployment in a given situation.

Managing Resources

- ✔ Create and manage local user accounts and local group accounts to meet given requirements.
- ✔ Set up and modify user profiles.
- ✔ Set up shared folders and permissions.
- ✔ Set permissions on NTFS partitions, folders, and files.
- ✔ Install and configure printers in a given environment.

Connectivity

- ✔ Add and configure the network components of Windows NT Workstation.
- ✔ Use various methods to access network resources.
- ✔ Implement Windows NT Workstation as a client in a NetWare environment.
- ✔ Use various configurations to install Windows NT Workstation as a TCP/IP client.
- ✔ Configure and install Dial-Up Networking in a given situation.
- ✔ Configure Microsoft Peer Web Services in a given situation.

Running Applications

- ✔ Start applications on Intel and RISC platforms in various operating system environments.
- ✔ Start applications at various priorities.

Monitoring and Optimization

- ✔ Monitor system performance by using various tools.
- ✔ Identify and resolve a given performance problem.
- ✔ Optimize system performance in various areas.

Troubleshooting

- ✔ Choose the appropriate course of action to take when the boot process fails.

- ✔ Choose the appropriate course of action to take when a print job fails.

- ✔ Choose the appropriate course of action to take when the installation process fails.

- ✔ Choose the appropriate course of action to take when an application fails.

- ✔ Choose the appropriate course of action to take when a user cannot access a resource.

- ✔ Modify the Registry using the appropriate tool in a given situation.

- ✔ Implement advanced techniques to resolve various problems.

Relating Microsoft's exam objectives to test preparation

Before actually constructing your study schedule, review the exam preparation guides and the *MCSE ...For Dummies* book that you plan to use. Each book in this series is aligned exactly with the objectives that correspond to the exam, so you don't have to filter through a lot of information that's not on the exam. You may notice early in the process that the exam preparation guides are not terribly specific. They look at various requirements in a general sense; but your study skills and the text have to pull all this information together. Use the objectives in the guides to help you prepare your schedule and your study of the appropriate *MCSE ...For Dummies* book.

Here's the list of exam objective categories. You can expect to find them scattered throughout this book, just as a gentle reminder of what each exam covers:

- ✔ Planning
- ✔ Installation and Configuration
- ✔ Managing Resources
- ✔ Connectivity
- ✔ Monitoring and Optimization
- ✔ Troubleshooting

Keep in mind that Official Curriculum and other Microsoft-approved study guides are not organized in an exam objective category manner, but in a chapter-by-chapter manner. For example, if you're studying for NT Workstation 4.0, a typical book offers at least one chapter on installation. Content from that chapter may cross several exam objective categories, such as Installation and Configuration and Troubleshooting. One big advantage to using the *MCSE ...For Dummies* books is that you don't have to sift through non-exam-specific content; the *MCSE ...For Dummies* books filters out the important stuff for you — and puts it together in a logical order.

Work your study schedule around the organization of the book. The amount of time that you devote to covering and *learning* a particular group of chapters is up to your good judgment because we all learn at different speeds. You have to give yourself enough time to develop comfort with the content, review the content, and, perhaps, revisit the content if you get bogged down in the technology — which happens to all of us, eventually.

Discovering that all exam objectives are not created equal

This section can help you avoid a major pitfall that many MCSE candidates don't see coming until they take a tumble. Although you need to review the exam objectives for any exam you're studying for, understand that not all exam objectives are created equal!

Here's what we mean: If you read the exam objectives, you naturally assume that the exam questions equally represent the six categories. In other words, for a 60-question exam, you may expect about 10 questions per category. But clever Microsoft doesn't fall for such simplicity.

The exam preparation guides are important, but they are just that — "guides." The actual exam questions are not equally distributed, and some of them may cross categories as well. For example, on a typical exam, the questions may break out percentage-wise as follows:

- Planning — 10%
- Installation and Configuration — 15%
- Managing Resources — 20%
- Connectivity — 25%
- Monitoring and Optimization — 20%
- Troubleshooting — 10%

The next exam's category percentages may be completely different. The point is, plan to review the exam objectives and the content listed in each objective, but don't worry too much about giving equal time to every objective.

Here's another tip that often distracts new test-takers. Say that you take the Networking Essentials exam and you pass on the first try (good for you!). You receive a printed report at the testing center that shows your score and the percentage of questions you answered correctly in each category. (Don't get too excited — it won't show you the questions, unfortunately.) When you pick up your Networking Essentials score sheet, here's what you see:

- ✔ Planning — 80%
- ✔ Installation and Configuration — 90%
- ✔ Managing Resources — 76%
- ✔ Connectivity — 50%
- ✔ Monitoring and Optimization — 73%
- ✔ Troubleshooting — 79%

When you first glance at this report, you may think, "Wow! I didn't do well on connectivity — I need to spend more study time on that area for future exams." Whoa! Not necessarily true. Why? What if the exam had only six questions on connectivity? You only missed three in that category — not enough to warrant great concern for future study on other exams. You really have no way of ever knowing how many exam questions are in each category, so be careful when trying to interpret the significance of the test report — it could actually throw your studies off track.

Before the exam ends, make a mental note of the kinds of questions you had trouble with. Then, if you happen to fail the exam (curses!), you have a more direct approach for tackling it again. (We explain additional tactics for managing the exam in Chapters 7 and 8.)

Assembling Your MCSE Study Plan

After you review the exam preparation guide, and you have your *MCSE ...For Dummies* book in hand, you're ready to map out a plan that focuses on organization and time.

We cannot emphasize enough the importance of getting plenty of rest, especially while you're studying for your MCSE exams. Your body needs a pause and your brain deserves some R & R. Nevertheless, when we study or write or become engrossed in a project, we often forget to do the most basic things: rest, eat, or even, stop. Although setting boundaries may seem almost ridiculous to bring up, it's not uncommon for people to experience MCSE burnout. You know the routine: You work too hard, then give up when you become overwhelmed. The key to avoiding burnout — MCSE-related or otherwise — is to balance your life.

So, produce that day-planner of yours and start making some daily plans. You're set to make the commitments necessary to pass the MCSE certification exams.

How you manage your study time is, of course, a personal decision. If you work full-time, your study schedule is likely to be different from the fortunate soul who has all day to hit the books. Overall, no matter what approach you choose, you have to devote several hours each day to your studies.

Also, you have to determine how many weeks of study are right for you *before* you attempt the exam, which, of course, depends on your work and study schedule. On average, the exams require 7 to 8 weeks of preparation. So balance your plan carefully, setting a realistic deadline that takes into account the amount of time you need to properly prepare for your exam.

Assume that you're self-studying for the Networking Essentials exam, and you decide to give yourself 6 weeks for study and another 2 weeks to pass the exam. The book you're using is 15 chapters long. Your overall study approach may look something like this:

- ✓ **Week 1:** Learn the first 3 chapters.

- ✓ **Week 2:** Focus on the next 4 chapters.

- ✓ **Week 3:** Cover the next 3 chapters; review the exam preparation guide to refocus on objectives.

- ✓ **Week 4:** Learn the next 2 chapters; try a midpoint assessment with one of the practice exams at the back of your *MCSE ...For Dummies* book and on the book's CD-ROM.

- ✓ **Week 5:** Check out the last 3 chapters; take a break for a day or two.

- ✓ **Week 6:** Review all your notes and preparation materials; try the practice exams at the back of the *MCSE ...For Dummies* book and on the CD-ROM.

- ✓ **Week 7 or 8:** Take the exam.

This schedule offers a general approach to the MCSE studies in a 7- to 8-week format. The next section helps you adapt your study time to the MCSE content and takes a look at a typical week.

Adapting Your Study Time to the MCSE Content

After you determine your available study time, and how you can manage that schedule, you have to examine all your study materials to determine the next logical step.

Avoid the "some sunny day" syndrome

The "some sunny day syndrome" affects many MCSE candidates. The first sign of a problem is the somewhat weakly pronounced promise, "I'll take the exam *next* week." You do need to study and practice, but at some point, you just have to try to pass the exam. If you don't pass the first time, the world doesn't end — but if you constantly put off the exams, the less likely you are to finish the MCSE.

This section lists our recommendations for creating study plans for a typical week. Use these suggestions as a guide for planning your own study schedules. As always, be flexible. Notice that we suggest that weekends remain free. This plan is hypothetical, of course; you can use it in any way you see fit.

This section presents a general daily approach for self-study. You have to tackle the material the first week to determine your progress and any adjustments that you may have to make. Assume that you're studying for the NT 4.0 Server exam. We propose covering three chapters the first week, following this plan:

- **Monday:** Read and take notes on Chapter 1. (In Chapter 5 of this book, we describe methods for taking effective notes.)

- **Tuesday:** Review your notes from Chapter 1 and take any quizzes provided in the book. Review any missed items. Read and outline Chapter 2.

- **Wednesday:** Review Chapter 1. Review the first half of Chapter 2 and quiz yourself on the content. Complete Chapter 2 and read half of Chapter 3.

- **Thursday:** Review Chapters 1 and 2. Quiz yourself on the first half of Chapter 3. At this point, your performance is pretty error-free on questions about the content in Chapters 1 and 2 (if not, consider a revisit to that material). Finish Chapter 3.

- **Friday:** Review Chapter 3 and take quizzes on that chapter. Test yourself on the content in Chapters 1 and 2. Write a test for yourself on the content from all three chapters and take the test!

Staying Focused on Your MCSE Study Goals

If the daily schedule we describe in the preceding section seems overwhelming, well, it is. Sometimes, you may feel like quitting. You're even likely to experience the urge to throw the computer out the window! And, as a last resort, you may decide to take up gardening. Is this normal? You betcha! Everybody gets frustrated. When you're working toward a goal, especially a goal that requires extreme dedication, the stress is going to be tremendous.

We want you to become an MCSE, just as we did. We've been where you are, and we know how it feels to want to toss in the towel.

When that happens, step back and do a reality check. Close the books. Go jogging. Do some gardening. Go to a movie. Take a soothing shower. Getting through the process requires creativity, patience, and an occasional flight of fancy. Try whatever works for you.

While you're studying for your exams, write FOCUS in big letters on a pad of those tiny, sticky notes. Then take the notes and post them randomly throughout your books and notes. As you plow through the pages, you'll suddenly stumble into one of those notes. Surprisingly, just seeing the word FOCUS can help to snap you back into consciousness. Try it!

Become a test writer

The Microsoft exams focus on specifics. Knowing the general information about the operating systems or concepts just won't cut it. You can test your comprehension of the fine points by becoming a test writer — for yourself! Pull tricky, little details from each chapter of your *MCSE ...For Dummies* book and write test questions. Then, take the test yourself. Because you wrote the test, you'll probably come up with the right answers, but the important part of the whole process has less to do with taking the test than it does with writing the practice exam. Writing detailed test questions can help you remember all that small stuff!

Chapter 5
Time to Tackle the Book

. . . .

. . . .

The moment finally arrives — and no excuse can hold you back from beginning your studies for the exam. In many ways, preparing for a Microsoft exam is like looking at a tall, treacherous mountain that you're committed to climb. You may hesitate to take the first step because you know the journey won't be easy. This chapter can help you set out on your trek by showing you how to study your *MCSE ...For Dummies* book and how to test your learning. Just keep your eyes on the summit and let the ascent begin!

Expecting, Perhaps, Gone With the Wind?

Unfortunately, studying and remembering the technical content you need to know to pass the Microsoft exams is not as much fun as reading a good novel. Yet, many candidates approach the MCSE study in this way — they read the book, spend a little time reviewing, then expect to ace the exam. For most of us, the process is not that easy.

The Microsoft exams are rigorous at best, and you really have to apply careful study and preparation to pull off a passing score. The wisest approach to digesting all that the book has to offer is to focus on chapter-by-chapter content, learning and reviewing the information as you go. Reading the book from start to finish with the intent to remember what you touched on lightly is not your best bet for exam success.

So, if studying for a Microsoft exam is not quite the same as traveling through the drama of *Gone With the Wind,* how should you proceed? Here's an outline of our recommended approach for tackling the *MCSE ...For Dummies* book for the exam you plan to take. We look at each of these steps in detail.

✔ Take the Quick Assessment at the beginning of the chapter. This test gives you a good idea of your current skills and what you have to learn.

✔ Read the chapter in a section-by-section manner, highlighting important points.

✔ Stop after each section and make notes on the terminology and passages that you highlighted. Practice any lab exercises on your computer.

✔ After you finish the chapter, re-read it, checking your notes for accuracy and making sure you haven't left out anything.

✔ Study the content. Memorize terminology and specific information.

✔ Review, and perform the Prep Test at the end of the chapter before moving on to the next chapter.

Reading the sections with highlighter in hand

Technical books typically provide a level of detail and jargon that can put you in a coma — or at least inspire you to a long nap. Consider approaching each chapter in sections — breaking down the coverage into palatable bites. This way, you're reading only a small amount of information at one time. Otherwise, no matter how disciplined or how interested you may be, or how well the book is written, you can expect your eyes to glaze over right before you begin daydreaming about your next vacation instead of figuring out network topology.

As you read the section, grab a good highlighter and note important terms or thoughts. But beware of falling prey to what many MCSEs refer to as "diarrhea of the highlighter" — a little gross maybe, but a point well taken. Highlight sparingly — don't highlight every other sentence.

Try to pull out the essence of the chapter so that the highlighted material has some focus and meaning. If you highlight half of the section, you're missing the most salient points.

Check out the following paragraph as an example:

> PPTP (Point to Point Tunneling Protocol) provides a method for transporting secure data over the Internet in a protocol other than TCP/IP. Many corporations that do not use TCP/IP on their local networks find this method an inexpensive and practical way to use the Internet to their advantage. PPTP allows the creation of a VPN (Virtual Private Network) between two sites. This virtual network is able to encapsulate, or hide, the local protocol, such as NetBEUI, inside of a PPP packet for transfer on the Internet. This way, the data appears to use PPP for Internet transmissions, although this is not the case.

Boy, wasn't that fun? Okay now, what deserves highlighting in that paragraph? Remember, you only want key terms or phrases. In the following paragraph, we propose a highlighting plan — look for the bold type:

> **PPTP (Point to Point Tunneling Protocol) provides a method for transporting secure data over the Internet in a protocol other than TCP/IP.** Many corporations that do not use TCP/IP on their local networks find this method an inexpensive and practical way to use the Internet to their advantage. PPTP allows the **creation of a VPN (Virtual Private Network)** between two sites. This virtual network is able to **encapsulate, or hide, the local protocol**, such as NetBEUI, inside of a PPP packet for transfer on the Internet. This way, the data appears to use PPP for Internet transmissions, although this is not the case.

The highlighted sections catch the key terms, thoughts, and definitions. Because no other specific information appears in this paragraph, the bold-faced phrases are all you need.

Avoid highlighting general ideas and thoughts that you can remember on your own; use the highlighter to point out the details.

Taking notes

After you read a section and highlight the important points and terminology, take time to stop and make a few notes. You may wonder, what's the purpose of taking notes if you're using a highlighter anyway? The notes you create are the basis of what you will study when you finish with the book. The highlighted sections are your guide to writing notes. After you close the book, you're ready to move to your notes and practice exams to continue your study.

The pen is mightier than the highlighter

Many people avoid taking notes because it's time-consuming. They assume that they can breeze back through the book and review all those highlighted passages as a final review. This approach usually doesn't work well — the material is too disconnected and you end up rereading sections you don't understand because you're missing context. Notes enable you to synthesize your highlighted portions into a user-friendly study preparation.

The highlighted sections guide your notetaking — they're not a study aid on their own. Taking notes causes you to repeat information, which can lead to learning the material. Making yourself rewrite the technical content in your own words does wonders for helping you remember the details — and it also makes review much easier.

If you stop to take notes at the end of each section rather than at the end of the chapter, you're less likely to leave out important information, and you stand a better chance of winding up with detailed notes.

As a part of the notetaking process, use your computer to try out the material that you find in each section, if applicable to the subject you're studying. Hands-on experience may be difficult to achieve on exams such as Networking Essentials or NT Server 4.0 in the Enterprise, but for the operating system exams, TCP/IP, and the elective exams, you can find no substitute for seeing in real life what you read in a book. You can reinforce your understanding of the content presented in each section and also clear up any fuzzy areas you may have. As an example, revisit our highlighted paragraph from the preceding section in this chapter:

> **PPTP (Point to Point Tunneling Protocol) provides a method for transporting secure data over the Internet in a protocol other than TCP/IP.** Many corporations that do not use TCP/IP on their local networks find this method an inexpensive and practical way to use the Internet to their advantage. PPTP allows the **creation of a VPN (Virtual Private Network)** between two sites. This virtual network is able to **encapsulate, or hide, the local protocol**, such as NetBEUI, inside of a PPP packet for transfer on the Internet. This way, the data appears to use PPP for Internet transmissions, although this is not the case.

From your highlighted information and your general knowledge from reading, you're ready to make some notes. No great formula exists for taking notes. Some people like to organize the information into an outline, whereas others prefer to just use phrases. Go with your personal preference — whatever works for you.

Half-hour miracles

After you finish reading, highlighting, and taking notes on each chapter, give yourself a half-hour break before rereading the chapter. Do something fun, take a walk, get out of the house — anything nontechnical. Then, in half an hour, return to the book and reread the chapter. This half-hour break is just enough time for your brain to recoup and pull together the pieces. You may be amazed at the difference a half-hour can make!

Your notes on the highlighted paragraph may look something like this:

> PPTP — Point to Tunneling Protocol — transports secure data over Internet using a VPN — Virtual Private Network. It hides the network protocol and makes it look like PPP for Internet traffic.

That's all there is to it. Notice that the note is not too short, but it's not too long either. Most importantly, the synopsis makes sense to the writer. By successfully nailing down this concept, you don't have to come back to this section and reread it later.

Some people choose to create an additional page in their notes where they list all acronyms and definitions, such as PPTP. You end up with all terminology on one or two pages for quick reference. You may find this method useful as well. The exams use a plethora of acronyms without providing their meanings, so you do have to memorize them.

Conducting a chapter check

After you finish the last section of a chapter and take your notes, you may want to reread the chapter, which serves two purposes.

First, rereading helps you pull together the major concept of the whole chapter. Because you looked at the chapter in pieces the first time, the re-read helps you get the "big picture" firmly implanted in your mind.

Second, when reading, highlighting, and taking notes, you may to leave out an important detail or two. Distractions, fatigue, and a number of other contributing factors can cause you to miss important points. It's hardly uncommon to hear someone say, "I can't believe I missed that the first time." So reread to make sure you have it all!

Studying chapters

After you have the chapter under your belt, you come to the fun part. The time is ripe for studying your notes and working on memorizing acronyms and content.

Do not wait until you finish the book to study! The tendency is to postpone study until after you get through all the content: not a good plan. The material becomes more technical and more difficult as you progress, so you're better off stopping to study as you go — with an occasional pause to smell the roses, or the coffee, depending on which comes closer to keeping you on track.

If you're using an *MCSE ...For Dummies* book, each chapter gives you tips about what to memorize and pay careful attention to when you study. Make sure that you take note of these suggestions — the authors of these books have all been in your shoes before!

Each Microsoft exam expects you to concentrate on three major areas: concepts, procedures, and terms and acronyms. To properly prepare for your exam, set your study sights on the following categories of testable information:

Knowing concepts

A *concept* is information that tells you about a process or how something works. Concepts tend to be theoretical rather than hands-on. A good example is global and local groups in NT. The difference between global and local groups can be confusing, especially if you don't understand the concept that distinguishes the two. Local groups apply to resources, and global groups are users. Global groups can be given permission to "use" a local group — that is, to use the local resource. When you understand the concept, you can usually move on.

Putting procedures into perspective

The second focus for study involves procedures, which are activities that you may do on your computer, or at least have to understand and follow through from the book's content. For example, the NT Server exam may ask you how to promote a BDC to a PDC. To answer correctly, you need to know the steps in the user interface and the possible problems or issues associated with taking that action.

You can always master procedures faster if you can practice them on a computer.

Tackling terms and acronyms

No certification exam is complete without a few — or more — terms and acronyms. You may have to know if NT is DDE or OLE, or you may face telling the difference between WAN technology such as ATM, SONET, and FDDI. You get the point. Unfortunately, no one has invented an easy way to remember these sets of letters — you simply have to memorize them, because the exam won't cut you any slack. But never fear — methods are available to conquer Microsoft's beloved acronyms, which we talk about in the section "Revealing a Few Tricks of the Study Trade," later in this chapter.

Making the most of review and self-assessment

In a natural progression, self-assessment follows chapter completion and your study of that chapter's content. Just before you take a test, you can try some major self-assessment exams and other tricks available in the *MCSE ...For Dummies* books. (We also talk about these techniques in Chapter 6.) And, at the end of each chapter, you need to perform a brief self-assessment to see how you're doing. Here's why:

- ✔ The self-assessment can point out any deficiencies you may have so that you can review that section in the book or in your notes before moving on.

- ✔ The self-assessment can tell you if you really have the knowledge you need. You may ace a self-assessment for one chapter, then completely bomb a Prep Test later in your studies. Some days, no matter how hard we try, we just can't absorb all the information. Problems, stress, and physical fatigue can get the best of anyone. So don't be surprised if you just don't get it. The self-assessment gives you a clear clue that you need to stop and regroup before plowing ahead.

So how do you perform a self-assessment? We recommend three exercises. They're short, they're easy, and they can detect whether you know the content.

First, if you're using an *MCSE ...For Dummies* book, rely on the Prep Test assessment questions at the end of each chapter. Gauge the results and then review anything you miss by returning to the book or your notes.

To define and not to define

The Microsoft exams aren't designed to test you on the definitions of terms or acronyms. For example, you may find a question that involves what PPTP does, but you're not likely to encounter any requests for a true definition of the acronym itself.

Secondly, use your notes to write at least 15 questions for yourself. Then answer the questions. Try to ask questions on the most important content. For example, remember our paragraph about PPTP, earlier in this chapter? Here are suggested questions on that content (can you answer them?):

- What is PPTP?
- What kind of network is created by using PPTP?
- What is the advantage of using PPTP?

How did you do? The questions are simple, but they do test your knowledge of the content. Here are the answers:

- PPTP is Point to Point Tunneling Protocol.
- You create a Virtual Private Network (VPN) by using PPTP.
- The advantage of using PPTP is that you can send LAN traffic over the Internet without the high cost of private connections.

Finally, after you pass the book's Prep Test and your own test, ask a family member or friend to give you an oral exam. Hand over your notes so that your helper can pose questions from the material you consider most important — and mix up the content to make sure you've got it!

Revealing a Few Tricks of the Study Trade

Make no bones about it, Microsoft exams are difficult, and mastering the content you need to know to pass is no minor undertaking. So, you're comfortable managing the chapter and the sections, but how do you go about understanding and memorizing all this stuff? Good tactics reach beyond just staring at your notes. Here are a few of the more effective ones.

Presenting great memorization magic

Some people find memorization tricks helpful, such as creating rhymes or extended meanings for an acronym to help jog the memory during the exam. Some people like to use mnemonics for complicated memorization, such as the seven layers of the OSI model.

A *mnemonic* is an association that helps you remember an acronym or process order. For example, the seven layers of the OSI model are Application, Presentation, Session, Transport, Network, Data Link, and Physical. To remember the order of the pieces, you can invent a mnemonic such as "**A**ll **P**eople **S**eem **T**o **N**eed **D**ata **P**rocessing."

Be advised, however, that these tricks don't work for everyone. If you have a tendency to remember the mnemonic but forget what it actually represents, we suggest that you find another way to call forth information when you're under pressure to show what you know.

Pulling flash cards out of the hat

You may find the use of flash cards helpful when you study terms and acronyms. This study tool works for us.

Before you start having flashbacks to fifth-grade math class, know that these quick-response cards translate well to adult education for a couple of reasons. First, you have to make them. The creation of flash cards helps familiarize you with the material.

Secondly, flash cards mix the terms up so that you have to do more than memorize an "order." For example, if you have 15 Networking Essentials terms written on a sheet of paper, you can memorize the list and say them over and over. But can you say them out of that particular sequence? Many times, the answer is no — and the exams are very good about confusing you, so memorizing an order list is a bad idea. Flash cards remove this stumbling block because they mix the order every time you use them (unless, of course, you keep them in order on purpose — which defeats the whole purpose).

Writing your way to instant recall

Speaking of writing out flash cards, putting pen to paper helps many people not only remember acronyms and terms but also recall general content (please, no disappearing ink). We like to organize terms and even general content, then start rewriting, and rewriting, and rewriting . . . and eventually, we no longer need notes because the details are now almost second nature. Time-consuming? Perhaps, but then again, the investment is worthwhile if it works for you.

The trick to making the writing technique work without consuming too much time is to put your notes in your own words — do not copy notes from the book.

Recording the moment on tape

Here's another tactic that many people use with terms, acronyms, and general content: Get a tape recorder and recite all the vital information onto a cassette. Then, you can listen to the tape over and over in the car or while you're taking care of mundane tasks at home. Many people swear by this tactic, but beware: Living with you and listening to your tape may cause pain, misery, and even mass exodus among nontechnical family members who don't have such a keen appetite for understanding the intricacies of FAT32 file systems or Serial Line Internet Protocol.

Directing your attention to the bizarre and the strange

You can invent all kinds of other schemes to support your exam preparation efforts, some of them oddly interesting. Here are a few imaginative ideas:

- ✔ We've heard of people covering one whole wall in their living rooms with butcher paper, then painting every piece of information about the exam on the paper. By the time they finish their masterpiece — while watching Monday Night Football — they know every MCSE play for the exam.

- ✔ If you're a musician, write a song or two about your study material content and sing it over and over. Many people can learn things almost immediately if the information's set to music (but don't expect a Top 40 hit).

- ✔ Plan a lesson and teach the material to yourself on videotape, then watch it over and over (which can be rather unnerving — just don't worry about how much weight television adds to your appearance).

The point is, you can discover or create lots of ways to learn information and to conquer the Microsoft exams — you may have to count on your creativity. Don't worry about right or wrongs here; just do what works!

Figuring Out What Works for You

At the risk of presenting what may seem like a treatise from a graduate education class, we offer a serious point. We all assimilate information in different ways. No single study suggestion can work for everybody, but the odds are great that you can find an approach that fits your style. So which ones are for you?

To answer that question, you have to know if you are an auditory or visual learner. Most of us fall heavily into one category. If you're a visual learner, you may achieve the best results by creating flash cards, designing charts, graphs, or pictures, or writing notes over and over. Visual learners can hear a subject described or discussed all day and, without notes to use, are likely to forget every spoken word. Auditory learners need to hear it. The more they can hear, the better they learn. For these folks, the tape recorder is like a gold mine.

So which are you — a visual or auditory learner? You probably have a good idea already, but here's a simple test. On your way to work, put your radio on a half-hour news show. When you get to your place of employment, try to write down or repeat most of what the reporters said. If you can do it, you're probably an auditory learner. If you can hit only the high points, you're probably a visual learner.

If you're an auditory learner, rely on the study tactics that are auditory; if you're more visual, stay within that learning style. After all, this book's all about giving you a big edge for the Microsoft exams, and just knowing how you learn best can make a major contribution to your MCSE success!

Chapter 6

Reviewing and Practicing

- -

In This Chapter

▶ Knowing your notes by heart

▶ Designing your own practice exam

▶ Practicing test-taking via other resources

▶ Making note of your exam results

▶ Looking for certification support in all the right places

- -

*T*he glorious day looms large on your calendar. You're now best friends with your *MCSE ...For Dummies* book (or, at least, close companions), you know the Microsoft exam preparation guide as well as your Social Security number, and you're looking forward to claiming victory on your certification exam. You're well on the road to conquering that proverbial mountain, but you know that the last stretch of the climb is probably going to be the most difficult. Before you set foot in the exam center, you need to put together all the information you've collected in preparation for the exam. This chapter shows you how to perform your final review and how to use practice exams to pinpoint, study, and learn sneaky content.

Reviewing Your Notes

If you've taken good notes along the way, you no doubt have a pile of paper staring at you by now. Hopefully, you've dutifully studied and memorized along the way, which will make your final review less than a monstrous task. If you somehow managed to miss the importance of a consistent study plan, then you need to backtrack and get busy with your notes before you try to tackle a practice exam.

Facing another writing session

Organization can make or break your notes. Ideally, when we study and take notes, we produce neat little packages that make perfect sense and are in perfect order. For most of us, that scenario is but a fantasy. As we study, we take our notes, then add bits and pieces to them, and continue to plug in even more information as we really start to understand the content. A wise move is to spread all your notes out on one big table, and rewrite them — again.

This action accomplishes two goals. The first, of course, is organizing everything neatly so that you can continue to review. As you rewrite, focus particular attention on the following tasks:

- ✔ Collect all the information on one topic. You may have different notes on the same subject — pieces of information that you picked up along the way. For example, if you're studying for Networking Essentials, put everything about 10BaseT networks on the same page.

- ✔ Make your notes neat, organized, and clearly legible — nothing's worse than trying to translate your own writing as you run through last-minute review. Use bullet points and numbered lists so that you can scan the information without getting stuck in a pile of words.

- ✔ Number your notes pages so that the order's completely clear. This task may seem mundane, but pages of notes are often hard to put back in order without page numbers.

Rewriting accomplishes a second goal. Rewriting your notes a final time helps you remember everything you've learned. All those bits of information represent a big summary, of sorts, and the rewrite can reinforce your recall so that you can answer those exam questions without hesitation.

Working out with those notes until it hurts

The next part of reviewing your notes is, well, reviewing. Now is the time to read through your notes and remember concepts and terms that you've encountered before. This review is an ongoing process that you need to do several times a day until you take the test. We suggest you begin by reading your notes three times in a row, seeing if you can remember the content and have a full understanding. As you do this, three things are likely to happen:

- ✔ You develop comfort with most of the content. You understand the content and feel good about seeing familiar material on the exam.

- ✔ You probably come across some pieces of content that you just don't get. You can read the notes, but something just doesn't gel. You need to pull the book out again and reread those sections to make sure you're comfortable with the content, and you understand it.

- ✔ A few terms or phrases confuse you every time you read your notes. Grab your trusty highlighter and make those terms or phrases stand out so that you can concentrate on them. Rewrite the definition so that it makes sense to you! Also, try to use a comparison to help you remember the term. For example, a database is a like a brick wall — each piece of data fits in a certain place in an orderly fashion.

Active rewriting

When you're rewriting your notes, be sure that you're actively involved in the effort — which doesn't mean watching TV at the same time. Instead, treat the rewrite just like you would a study session. Remember, the goal is to learn as you write!

After your initial read, keep going over your notes again and again — several times a day. When is enough "enough"? When you absolutely hate every word in your notes, feel free to move on to a practice exam. We know from experience that college speech and debate teams are instructed to memorize their presentations because no notes are allowed in tournaments. As more than one speech coach has said, "You're not ready to present your speech until you hate every word of it." Your study notes are the same — when you hate to read them, you probably know them well.

Studying your notes is a continual process — not something you do one evening. Plan to review them up until the day before the exam.

Putting together a cheat sheet

After you spend ample time reviewing your notes, you have one more action to complete: creating a cheat sheet. No, we're not talking about traditional crib notes that you sneak into the exam with you, although in a sense, that's exactly what you're going to do — only legally. You tuck this cheat sheet, however, away in your brain instead of your pocket.

Here's what you do: Pull out the acronyms, key terms, and information that you need to know cold. Of course, each exam differs in its content, but the Networking Essentials and TCP/IP tests require you to memorize a number of terms and even mathematical formulas for the exam — no way around the truth, you simply have to know them verbatim.

To help you get ready for the exams, the *MCSE ...For Dummies* books point out the key ideas or formulas you have to memorize. Also, each *MCSE ...For Dummies* book comes with a cheat sheet that highlights key points.

Get all your vital information together before you begin creating your cheat sheet; you don't want to spend time searching or writing over and over while you're trying to develop this important tool.

Now, take a sheet of plain white paper and draw a grid of 12 blocks. In each block, write out information that you need to memorize. For example, if you're taking the Networking Essentials exam, put the OSI model in one block, information about the 10Base*x* networks in another block, information about the WAN technologies such as SONET, FDDI, ATM, and so on.

Use a white, $8^1/_2$ x 11 sheet of paper, the same sort as you can expect to receive for scratch paper at the exam center. You want the cheat sheet to look exactly the same, even down to the kind of paper.

After you put all the information on the cheat sheet, you can start memorizing it, working on learning each block of information. When you think you know the page, put it away, take a clean sheet of typing paper, and try to exactly re-create the sheet from memory. Messing up the first time is no big deal; just continue practicing until you can re-create the cheat sheet every time you try without any errors.

Now you have your own cheat sheet in your memory. At the exam center, you're given scratch paper. Before you start the exam, you can simply re-create your own cheat sheet — perfectly acceptable to the test proctors. This way, you have the information for reference while you take the test. The test won't hesitate to try to confuse you (and the test, we might add, is quite good at it). But with your own cheat sheet at your side, you're sure to get the right answers. And, you're not breaking any rules!

Creating a Practice Exam

When you hate your notes and you can write your own cheat sheet from memory, the time is right to create a practice exam for yourself. We recommend that you write a short-answer test on everything that appears in your notes. Don't be surprised if your exam is somewhat lengthy, and you take quite a lot of time writing an answer to every question.

All Microsoft exams are multiple choice, but we recommend that you write a short-answer test for yourself because this kind of assessment is more difficult. If you can answer the questions in a short-answer format, you're more likely to score well with the multiple choice questions on the exam.

The best approach is to write the exam and put it aside for a day or two, then return to the exam and take the exam at one sitting without any help from your notes. You can then get a clear picture of what you need to emphasize in your studies.

Write a variety of questions, but make sure that your questions focus on details and require detailed responses. The real exam focuses on specifics — not broad concepts.

Your friend, your spouse, your children as exam-writing partners

You don't have to be technically astute to write an exam for someone else. If your notes are well-written, ask a friend or family member to design a bunch of short-answer questions for you.

Taking Practice Exams

If you survive your own practice exam, see what you can do with the professional models. Each *MCSE ...For Dummies* book provides at least one practice exam in the "Appendixes" section. The CD-ROM that's customized for every book contains additional samples of practice exams that are available from other companies, such as Transcender. The *MCSE ...For Dummies* CD-ROMs even contain a game to test your knowledge — try it, it's fun! You may choose to purchase practice exam software that simulates the real Microsoft test — a wise investment.

The electronic practice exams give you a time limit, just like you'll face on the actual exam. Take the exam at one sitting, without the use of your notes, and try to finish the exam within the time limit. Answering and thinking quickly is a basic requirement of any MCSE exam.

When the time's up, you receive a score and have an opportunity to review what you missed. If you're taking a third-party exam, such as those offered by Transcender, don't fret if you don't score as well as you'd hoped. The practice exams are often more difficult than the real exam. Generally, if you score from 600 to 700, you're in pretty good shape.

If your score is very low, you need to do some additional study. You can work more with your notes and apply more effort to memorization, and you can also use the exam results to create more notes, which we cover in the next section.

Picking Up Clues from Practice Exam Results

Practice exams not only provide opportunity to practice taking the test but also share valuable information that you can add to your notes. The practice exam often points out some detail or concept that you haven't paid much attention to.

After you take a practice exam, review the exam results, focusing on the questions you missed and the correct answers. Most practice exams give you a short explanation of why the answer is correct. After you review the exam results, go back through the exams and take some additional notes on the questions you answered incorrectly. If you missed a question because you somehow stumbled over the answer options, but you understand the answer, you don't have to worry about a note for that question. But when you see terms or concepts that are foreign to your studies, treat the information like pure gold — these gems provide tips and hints about the real exam.

The practice exams are simply study tools, not an exact measure of your expected performance on the real exam. Taking the practice results too seriously may either defeat your confidence or possibly, overinflate it. Just keep in mind that these resources are not accurate measures of your knowledge and skill.

Tapping Additional Certification Study Resources

This section takes you into that wild, free-for-all territory of additional resources. These resources can help you find out more about particular exams, or MCSE certification and the information technology field in general.

Many of these resources are free, mostly available through the Internet. Others can be quite costly. Information technology isn't a cheap career choice. However, we're convinced that you can become an MCSE without getting a second mortgage.

The good news is that you can choose from an enormous amount of additional resources. The bad news is that some of these resources are terrific and some are, well, not so hot. That's a judgment call you'll have to make as you research and collect these resources.

The URLs for Internet resources may change from time to time. If you cannot reach the resource from the addresses provided, try looking for the resource through any search engine.

Discovering the marvels of TechNet

Does your budget limit what you can buy? And do you want to make sure that you get the best resource you can find? Then check out TechNet. In fact, even if you do buy third-party materials, becoming familiar with TechNet is one of the wiser investments of your time and money.

TechNet is a support tool that features articles, white papers, and technical documentation on all Microsoft products. In the industry, TechNet is the bible when it comes to the most up-to-date information on any Microsoft product.

Incidentally, if you don't have Internet access, or want to talk to a person, the telephone number for TechNet is 800-344-2121.

Microsoft considers TechNet as reliable and meaningful to study as the Official Curriculum.

Microsoft makes TechNet available in two ways:

✔ TechNet is available free-of-charge online, through the Microsoft Web site. This version is what Microsoft calls a "subset," which means that the information is scaled down, with less scope than the CD version. You can visit TechNet online, as shown in Figure 6-1, at:

```
www.microsoft.com/technet
```

Figure 6-1: TechNet online is the best MCSE researching resource.

Free TechNet

You can get a free, trial copy of the TechNet CD from Microsoft. This sample is a full working copy in every way.

Microsoft TechNet ITHome — Free Trial:

```
204.118.129.122/giftsub/
        clt1Form.asp
```

When you get to this page, access the *IT Resources, Technet Reference* headings by clicking the link in the left column.

If you use the online TechNet, you can sign up for a newsletter called the *TechNet LISTSERV.* Sent to your e-mail address every two weeks, the *TechNet LISTSERV* notifies you of updates to the TechNet Web site.

✔ You can buy a CD subscription for a full year for around $300. The CD subscription is broader in scope, while the online support site represents major information components. The CD version contains resource kits, drivers, patches, and a lot of stuff that is convenient to have on CD. To order a subscription to TechNet, go to:

```
www.microsoft.com/ithome/orderTN
```

One benefit of becoming an MCSE is a free, one-year subscription to TechNet. You also get TechNet online as part of the MCSE Web site. If you choose to purchase the full CD version of TechNet before you finish your certification, don't worry, Microsoft will extend your subscription to make certain you get one year free.

In late summer 1998, Microsoft made a major commitment to expanding the TechNet program. In addition to the Web site and the subscription CD program, Microsoft now offers TechNet briefings.

TechNet briefings are free seminars, featuring Microsoft employees as speakers, that are presented live around the country. You can find out if and when a seminar is in your area by going to the TechNet Web site. And if you have a question about TechNet, write Microsoft at technet@microsoft.com.

If you can afford it, get TechNet. If not, use the online resource. Whichever makes more sense for your situation, just remember our erstwhile advice: Use TechNet.

Finding a local MCSE user group

A user group is similar to a study group in the sense that participants gather regularly to discuss issues related to MCSE exams. However, a user group is a bit more formal, larger, and in some instances, may charge you a fee for membership.

The best way to find a group is to ask somebody. The second way is to pick up one of those local computer magazines. In the bookstores in our locales, these free publications are stacked near the entrance. User groups are usually listed somewhere in the magazine. The listing contains a contact name, phone number, meeting times and place, and probably a Web page address.

You can also find these groups online. For instance, America Online lists all kinds of organizations. You can access these areas by clicking the Local button on the Channels menu. This action brings up the Digital City page, where you locate your geographical area on a map of the United States. Then, you select the Local Links option, followed by the Computers & Internet option. You'll probably find on the list any available group in your area.

Finding a local user group depends on your location. If you live in a large city, you're likely to find numerous groups. In fact, you may discover special interest user groups like Exchange Administrator Groups and MCSE and MCSD groups.

You can also do an online search by going to Yahoo (`www.yahoo.com`) or the search engine of your choice, and typing in a keyword search string like

```
Your cityname mcse user group
```

Use your expertise at cruising the Internet to refine your search as you go.

Searching out an online MCSE user group

The previous section offers an online method for finding a local user group. You can use this same method to find online groups.

The Saluki MCP Web page is more than an excellent resource with online chats, bulletin boards, and references; these folks also run a pretty nifty and very active Internet e-mail mailing list — a great example of an online user group for MCSE studies and related topics. The Saluki list supports a frank discussion between users. Often, you're able to find another user or users who agree to mentor you through the certification process.

The list, or at least the entry point, is located at:

```
www.saluki.com/mcp
```

Follow the link and read the information about the list on this page. To subscribe, send an e-mail message to:

```
majordomo@saluki.com
```

In the body of the message write:

```
SUBSCRIBE mcse your e-mail address@domain name
```

You receive a subscription verification as well as a second e-mail message outlining various online rules and other news.

Saluki recently added a second list for MCSE technical questions. To subscribe, send an e-mail message to: `majordomo@saluki.com`.

In the body of the message, include this text:

```
subscribe mcsetech your e-mail address@domain name
```

You receive a warning about receiving a lot of e-mail when you sign up for this list. They're not kidding! Often, you can have 50 to 100 or more e-mail messages as users take on a topic. So beware, and make sure that you have an ISP that can handle that volume of mail.

If you have any questions about Saluki, write to Scott Armstrong at `saluki@gate.net` or Dean Klug at `deano@gate.net`.

Here's another site of useful links:

```
www.magicnet.net/~noles/links.html
```

This site gives you important links for Microsoft testing information and additional information about a number of the exams, such as Networking Essentials and NT Server.

Navigating toward Microsoft newsgroups

By pointing your Internet news-reading software to the NNTP news server at Microsoft, you can read ongoing news, questions, answers, and comments on dozens of topics close to Microsoft products. The URL for the Microsoft Public NNTP server is `msnews.microsoft.com`, where you can direct your inquiries about Microsoft newsgroups.

Signing up for Microsoft mailing lists

You can sign up for a slew of Microsoft newsletters, which are automatically delivered to your mailbox. At the time of this book's publication, the newsletters included the following:

- BackOffice News
- Education Business Partner News
- Exclusive Preferred Member Update
- Exploring Windows
- MCP News Flash
- Microsoft Direct Access News
- Microsoft FrontPage Bulletin
- Microsoft Games Monthly Mailer
- Microsoft K-12 Connection
- Microsoft Press Book Connection
- Microsoft Press Pass
- Microsoft Seminar Online News Flash
- Microsoft Technical Support News Flash — BackOffice
- Microsoft Technical Support News Flash — Games, Reference & Kids' Products
- Microsoft Technical Support News Flash — Office
- Microsoft Technical Support News Flash — Windows and Internet Explorer
- Microsoft: This Week!
- MSDN Flash
- Office Enterprise Insider
- Office News Service
- "Smallbiz" News Flash
- TechNet Flash
- Technology Source for Higher Education
- Training and Certification News
- Windows CE Wire
- Windows NT Platform News

To subscribe, go to `register.microsoft.com/regwiz/` `personalinfo.asp`.

Subscriptions are a great way to keep up on *everything* that is new coming out of Microsoft. It really saves you time also because you don't have to visit the Web site to search for stuff.

Linking to MCSE-related Web sites

We'll point you in the right direction to find online information about MCSE. It's just too simple: Go to your favorite search engine — Yahoo!, Infoseek, Alta Vista, or any other you particularly respect — and type in **MCSE**. Prepare to register amazement at how much stuff is out there.

Securing a subscription to MCP Magazine

You can find magazines galore on MCSE certification and related topics, but we highly recommend *MCP Magazine*. As Microsoft's official MCP publication, this magazine keeps you abreast of what's going on in the certification world.

You receive a free one-year subscription to *MCP Magazine* after you become an MCP.

You can find out more about the magazine via any of these connections:

- Internet: `www.mcpmag.com`
- Fax: 714-863-1680
- Mail: MCP Magazine, 1500 Quail Street, 6th Floor, Newport Beach, CA 92660
- Phone: USA 800-780-2897; outside the USA 815-734-1282

MCP Magazine reviews all training materials, so be sure to check out its online archives.

For a look at a list, and sometimes a review, of available third-party study materials, go to `www.mcpmag.com/sendmeinfo`. You can also buy books at this site: `www.mcpmag.com/books`.

Putting Your Skills to the Test: Building a Home Computer Network

This book is as much about discovery as it is a list of actual things to do. If you really want to enjoy a great adventure while you prepare for your test-taking experience, consider building your own home network — a sure fire way to begin practicing many of the concepts you meet in classes or through self-study.

If you can afford to put together a home network, you need at least a server and a workstation computer — and the software for both. Evaluation copies of Windows NT Workstation and Windows NT Server are available for download at www.microsoft.com/msdownloads.

Trying your hand at home networking may provide lots of learning opportunities, especially because the undertaking is a pretty labor-intensive venture. If nothing else, you learn the basics of network architecture. For a full course in linking household computers, check out *Networking Home PCs For Dummies* by Kathy Ivens (IDG Books Worldwide, Inc.).

If your technical friends also have networks, try setting up Remote Access Server connections between your networks. Keep in mind that Connectivity is the category that generally registers the lowest exam scores.

We also recommend that you partition a few drives to be NTFS volumes, some to be FAT, and others as FAT32. Lots of interesting issues revolve around how these different permissions affect file-sharing — a likely candidate for some tough exam questions.

Buy it used

You can save a lot of money by buying used computers and network components. You may not have the most current CPU or hub, but hey, if it works and saves you money, you have made a wise choice. Check out the want ads in your local paper and even look for used hardware online — you'll save a bundle!

Part III

Conquering the MCSE Exams

The 5th Wave   By Rich Tennant

"He studies every available minute for his MCSE exam."

In this part . . .

*I*magine a perfect world: You study for an exam, become an expert on the topic, take the test, and pass with no problem, right? Well, you can dream on, but in Microsoft's world, the real deal is not so simple — or predictable. You know, of course, that you must study hard for the exams, but the testing experience is something that catches most new test-takers off guard. Microsoft's exams are somewhat unique, and you need some skills and knowledge about the exam and how it works to master it. Part III gives you the inside scoop on the Microsoft exams.

Chapter 7

Managing the Exam

● ●

In This Chapter

▶ Understanding the exam format

▶ Managing your time

▶ Using Item Review wisely

▶ Finding out your final score

● ●

*W*hat's the big deal? You go the testing center, you sit down at a computer, you take the test, and that's it. Not exactly. Before you attempt your first exam, you need a good idea about what to expect during the actual test experience. Also, we suggest that you go in with a certain understanding about what to do — and what not to do — when you take the exam. This chapter explains how to manage the exam and avoid some major mistakes that test-takers often make.

Clearing the Air about How the Exam Works

Microsoft exams somehow inspire a lot of confusion about what kind of test you can actually expect. Part of the puzzlement is because two major testing methods exist out there in the IT professional exam world: standard exams and adaptive exams. If you surf the Internet looking for information about how the Microsoft exams work and what kind of format you're likely to encounter, you can bet you'll discover a lot of stories. We're here to set the record straight so that you can stop worrying about the exam, and especially, so that you're not misled by faulty information.

Microsoft's use of standard exams

The great bulk of the Microsoft exams are standard exams, at least at this time. Here's what that means: First, you call Sylvan Prometric or Virtual University Enterprises (VUE), both official testing centers, to schedule an exam. Your complete registration (including payment by credit card) triggers downloading of a test to the exam center of your choice; attachment of your Social Security number makes the exam all your own. (To find out more about scheduling an exam, see Appendix A.)

The exam is one package, meaning it's a collection of "dumb" data, if you will. The questions that show up on the exam are determined before you walk into the testing center, and no matter how you answer the questions on the exam, you absolutely get that package of exam questions attached to your Social Security number. In other words, the test does not respond to how you answer the questions. These exams are "standard" exams — they work just like a paper exam that's prepared in advance.

Exams of the adaptive kind

In the land of information technology, you can also find another kind of test — the adaptive exam. Novell uses the adaptive testing method, and at the time of this writing, Microsoft is in the experimental phase of adaptive examinations. Adaptive exams are "smart" exams — they are able to understand your response to a question and judge whether you have answered the question correctly. If you don't answer a question correctly, you are usually given two or three follow-up questions on the same topic.

For example, if you're given a question about NTFS and you respond incorrectly, the exam knows that you missed the question, so it changes the exam path to give you more questions on this same topic. A little mean, don't you think? Also, adaptive exams normally do not allow you to change your answers at the end of the exam, and you can't move forward or backward through the exam. At the time of this writing, Microsoft is experimenting with adaptive tests for some of the core exams and some common electives, such as TCP/IP.

The reason we bring this whole point up is because of misinformation that you may see on the Internet. For example, the exams contain a short survey at the beginning that asks you questions about your certifications, your job, and so on. Many people think that if you make yourself appear to not know anything technical on the survey, your questions are going to be easier. This is not the case, and most tactics you find on the Internet telling you how to "trick" the adaptive exam do not work. The best advice, regardless of whether you get a standard exam or an adaptive exam, is to use the test-taking skills you learn in this book and the technical knowledge you gain in your *MCSE ...For Dummies* book.

Microsoft is not fully implementing adaptive testing at this time, but you may get an adaptive exam as you take some of the core exams. You can always keep abreast of any certification changes at www.microsoft.com/mcp or through *MCP Magazine*.

Bogus tactic watch

In general, be wary of exam advice that you may find on the Internet. You may come across a number of exam tactics, including such strange techniques as skipping all the exam questions, answering them instead in Item Review. (Item Review is an exam interface feature that enables you to review and change your answers.) The idea behind the bogus tactic is to skip all the questions, lock in the test set, and then change the answers during Item Review. Most of these tactics come from a fear of adaptive testing. They don't work and can easily throw your test-taking off track — not to mention that they waste a lot of your testing time.

Completing the Exam Survey

Each Microsoft exam contains a short, usually 15-question, survey at the beginning of the exam. Microsoft uses the survey for statistical purposes to gather information about who is taking the exams. Your responses on the survey do not impact the exam. That is, don't expect the exam questions to suddenly transform to an easier or more difficult series based on your survey responses.

The survey asks you questions about any previous certifications, what operating system you normally work with, your current occupation, and so on. Here's an important trick about the exam survey: You have an additional 15 minutes on top of your exam time to take the survey. However, you gain any unused survey time to use on the exam if you don't take 15 minutes to complete the exam.

In other words, the exam time (usually 90 minutes) and the survey time, usually (15 minutes) are combined. If you spend only 5 minutes answering the survey, you gain an additional 10 minutes for use on the exam — which is a lot when you're taking a test.

So, answer the survey, but do not ponder over it. Answer it quickly and get to the exam!

Working within Your Time Limit

The exam time limit is a major source of panic for most new test-takers — and it really doesn't have to be. The fact is, if you read at a normal rate and think at a normal rate, you have plenty of time to take the test. Most exams give you 90 minutes, plus any extra time you gain from the survey.

For some exams, an hour and a half is more than enough; for others, the allotted time is just enough. Some exams simply have more scenario-based questions that require a lot of reading. So, you wonder, which exams are difficult in terms of the time limit? Table 7-1 gives you an overview of the major exams and the inside scoop on the time limit.

Table 7-1	Time Limit Concerns per Exam
Exam	*Time Limit Concern*
Networking Essentials	You have to be careful on this exam. The scenario questions are often difficult and confusing and can consume a lot of time.
Windows 95	No problem — you have plenty of time.
Windows 98	No problem — you have plenty of time.
Windows NT Workstation	No problem — you have plenty of time.
Windows NT Server	No problem — you have plenty of time.
Windows NT in the Enterprise	This one is the worst. Most of the questions require reading a paragraph or two. You really have to watch your time limit.
TCP/IP	You have enough time, but do be cautious.
Internet Information Server	No problem — you have plenty of time.

So, some exams don't pose a problem while others may require you to cut it close. The best action for you to take is to develop a habit of looking at the time every 5 minutes. You find a clock at the upper right side of your screen, so just glance at the time every 5 minutes or so. An eye toward pace reduces the possibility of you looking up and having only 5 minutes to answer 20 remaining questions.

Working with the exam time limit is a skill just like anything else. The more exams you take, the better you become at managing the time. Unfortunately, the Networking Essentials exam, which we suggest is the first or one of the initial exams you take, can give you a run for your money. The trick is to keep your mind focused on the exam, but stay attuned to the time limit.

Working on a timed exam causes anxiety for many people. Use the practice exams to become accustomed to working within a time limit. You can figure out how fast you need to work to complete the exam on time, and you can look forward to less test anxiety on exam day.

Returning to Marked Questions

The exam allows you to "mark" questions. That is, a little check box appears in the upper left corner of the exam. If you click the check box, the question is "marked."

At the end of the exam, you're presented with an Item Review page that shows your answer to each question and highlights questions that you marked. At that time, you can double-click the question number and return to that question for further review.

So the question becomes, to mark or not to mark? At first glance, the answer seems to be a resounding, "Yes! Mark everything you're not certain of!" Wait a minute . . . that may not be the best tactic.

Marking everything that you don't know is usually a bad idea, mainly because different degrees exist in the broad range of "what I don't know." Consider the following question concerning Windows 98:

1 MSINFO contains viewers for which kind of file format?

   A ○ .txt

   B ○ .nfo

   C ○ .wlg

   D ○ MSINFO contains viewers for all of the above.

Okay, in this question, you have the choice of .txt, .nfo, and .wlg. You also have the option to select "D," which says MSINFO can read all three file types. You have to know the answer to the question. You have no way to work the question or play around with it to come up with the right answer — you either know it or you don't. If you get a question like this — and have no idea about the answer — go with your best guess rather than marking the question for review. For the curious, the correct answer to this question is D.

Don't expect exam questions to give away answers to other questions — it's just not going to happen in this lifetime. Many people mark questions in the hope that a later question may give away an answer to a question they don't know. Another question may jog your memory, but keep in mind that these exams are carefully developed. If you're absolutely stumped, your best bet is to make an educated guess and get away from the question. You don't want to spend additional time on it during Item Review.

So, if this is the case, which kind of question is a good candidate for marking? Consider this Networking Essentials example:

2 The degradation of a network signal as it travels on the cable is called:

A ○ Cross Talk
B ○ Attenuation
C ○ ATM
D ○ NNTP

In this example, you know that ATM, a type of WAN technology, and NNTP, a protocol, are not the correct answers. However, you argue with yourself over Cross Talk and Attenuation — you just can't make up your mind. When you wrestle between two answer choices, make your best guess, mark the question, then come back and look at it again in Item Review. Your brain will keep working on the question as you take the rest of the test, and when you look at it again, you may be able to come up with the right answer. By the way, the correct answer to the question is B.

Only mark questions that you have a good chance of answering correctly in Item Review. Do not mark questions that are completely foreign to you. Your best approach is to guess on those questions and not return to them. In a typical exam, you can expect to have five to seven questions marked for Item Review.

Answer every question as you move through the test — even questions that you mark. You may accidentally skip unanswered questions in your review, which will count against you. Also, if you happen to run out of time during Item Review, you can at least count on the possibility of stumbling into the correct answer.

Managing Item Review

An Item Review page appears after you answer the final exam question. You're able to see how you answered each question and review the marked questions. The "butterflies" usually kick in during Item Review because you're almost finished with the exam. Here's what you need to do during this important time.

First, scan the list to make sure that you haven't skipped any questions. Skipped questions are counted as "wrong" answers and will count against you in the score tabulation. A skipped answer shows only the question number, but no answer choice beside it. Double-click the number and you're taken back to that question so that you can answer it.

Don't skip questions, even those you mark. Make sure that you answer each question as you move through the exam.

Second, take a look at the marked questions. You can do this by double-clicking the question. At this time, you can keep your original answer or change the answer if you so desire.

Avoiding the "I Missed Them All" Syndrome

By the time you're in the middle of Item Review, those butterflies often turn to full-blown panic. Most test-takers have a tendency to second-guess all their answers, causing them to begin wading back through the exam during Item Review. Avoid this serious mistake.

Educational research tells us time and time again that your first answer is going to be your best answer. You don't want to start changing your answers after you finish the exam, when you're nervous about your score. At this point, you're not thinking clearly, and any changes you make usually yield disappointment. The fact is, if you change answers to questions (other than those you marked) during Item Review, you are highly likely to miss the right answer!

Use Item Review only to scan for skipped questions and to ponder the questions you've marked. Do not return to the other questions during Item Review.

Ending the Exam

The golden hour arrives. You're done with Item Review, the clock's ticking off your remaining time, and you're confident that you've given the exam your best shot. You're ready to end the exam.

You see a button at the bottom of your screen that says "End Review." After you click this button, you have an opportunity to offer feedback on the exam. For example, if you felt that question 27 was totally unfair, you can make a comment to that effect for Microsoft to see.

When you're satisfied that you've stated your case — which is completely voluntary — you click the End Exam button. At this point, you may want to hold your breath, but be forewarned, the computer may take 15 to 20 seconds to score the exam. You receive your results as a bar grid showing the passing score for the exam and your score. That's it!

Look closely at the bar graph presentation, especially if you're a frequent test-taker. Microsoft may flip-flop the order in which your score and the passing score appear.

The test administrator gives you a printed score report — complete with proctor's stamp — before you leave the testing center. Don't hesitate to request an extra copy — one for your records and one for a fitting gift to your current or future boss.

Now you can celebrate your success, or perhaps regroup to take the exam. Chapter 8 gives you a preview of what to expect on exam questions themselves, and Chapter 10 tells you what to do if you don't pass a test on the first try (after the tears).

Pre-exam planning

A good way to avoid "panic actions," such as changing answers just before the exam ends, is to decide ahead of time exactly what you're going to do during the exam, and then stick to those plans regardless of how you feel in the moment. You can say to yourself, "I am only going to change answers to marked questions during Item Review, and I will not look at other answers." Once you tell yourself this, stick to it — even if you feel a driving need to start tinkering with your first instinct.

Chapter 8

Managing the Exam Questions

. . . .

In This Chapter

▶ Identifying an assortment of exam question types

▶ Knowing how to approach any style of question

. . . .

*I*n this chapter, you find out how to manage the questions on the exam. In a sense, the exam is a game of odds, and anything you can do to increase your chances of coming up with the correct answer is a positive move. Of course, the best way to increase your odds is to study, study, study! But some additional tricks can help you to win this game. This chapter shows you what kinds of questions you're likely to see and how to tackle and logically "work" each kind of question.

Previewing the Kinds of Questions You're In For

If you use the practice exams provided in the *MCSE ...For Dummies* books as well as the prep tests offered by third parties, you can gain a good idea of the kinds of exam questions you're likely to encounter. The Microsoft exams are all based on multiple choice, with a few variations, of course. But at the core, all the questions ask you to choose one or more correct answers from a list of three to ten choices. Don't expect any short-answer formats and count on only an occasional True or False question. Generally, most of the questions ask you for the "best" answer and give you four choices to pick from.

Knowing what sorts of questions you're about to face before you tackle the test can make the exam experience a lot less unpredictable. The following sections give you a sample of the kinds of exam questions you're likely to see.

Looking forward to a load of simple multiple choice questions

Plan to see lots of simple multiple choice questions. The question stem usually presents you with a question that requires a "best" response.

The exam questions seldom ask you for the "best" response, but the exam assumes that you understand this approach. You may identify two answers that are technically correct, but you're expected to pick the "best" answer.

Here is a sample of a simple multiple choice question:

1 Which operating system can read an NTFS partition?

A ○ Windows 3.1
B ○ Windows 95
C ○ Windows NT
D ○ Macintosh

In a simple multiple choice question, you are expected to read the question and choose the correct or best answer. In this question, the only correct answer is C, Windows NT.

Fancying up the questions with complex multiple choice answers

Complex multiple choice questions function the same way as simple multiple choice. You're given a question stem and four answer choices. You're expected to select the correct or best answer. The difference with the complex multiple choice question is, well, it's complex. The answer stem is lengthy and the answer choices may involve several operations. Consider this example:

2 Janie wants to set up a dual-boot configuration with Windows 95 and Windows NT Workstation. The Windows 95 computer must be able to see the Windows NT partition. How should Janie establish the dual-boot configuration?

A ○ Windows 3.1
B ○ Windows 95
C ○ Windows NT
D ○ Macintosh

In this complex multiple choice question, you have to read the situation, understand the desired result, and then choose the action that will accomplish the desired result. In this question, the correct answer is B. The complex multiple choice questions can run from the depth of this example to question stems that are two to three paragraphs long, which are obviously a lot of fun.

Adding more challenge with Choose All That Apply questions

Choose All That Apply exam questions are among those most disliked by test-takers. In this kind of question, the exam gives a standard multiple choice stem, but instead of expecting the "best" answer, the test instructs you to choose all that apply, which means one correct answer or several. Often, Choose All That Apply questions have four answer choices, but no guarantees apply — they can have as many as seven. Consider this example:

3 Which protocols are a part of the TCP/IP protocol suite? (Choose all that apply.)

A ❑ SMTP
B ❑ NNTP
C ❑ IPX
D ❑ TCP

In this example, you're expected to choose all the correct answers, with the correct answers being A, B, and D. Choose All That Apply questions are difficult because you can't rule out any of the answers — all of them may be correct! But before you despair, know that later in this chapter we offer ideas on "Tackling multiple choice questions."

The rereading infinite loop

Test-takers commonly face a dilemma with complex multiple choice questions, especially if the question is two or three paragraphs long: We call the problem the "rereading infinite loop." By the time you get to the end of a question, you've forgotten what the whole discussion is even about, and you have to reread. You can avoid the rereading infinite loop by jotting down a few notes on your scratch paper as you read — a perfectly legal source of support.

Expecting you to choose three

A close cousin of the Choose All That Apply questions are the "Choose Three" (or any number, but often that number is three). Microsoft uses this kind of question more often than Choose All That Apply, so expect to see a few of these. In most cases, a Choose Three question gives you six or seven answer choices, as shown in this example:

4 Which TCP/IP utilities can be used to gain IP addressing information and statistics? (Choose three.)

A ❑ Iparp -d
B ❑ Ipconfig
C ❑ Ipstatc
D ❑ Netstat
E ❑ Tcpconfig
F ❑ Cstat -d
G ❑ Nbtstat

In this example, you pick the three correct answers, which are B, D, and G. Although Choose Three questions are similar to Choose All That Apply, they tend to be easier because you have a set number to pick rather than any number of combinations.

Posing a What Is The Result? puzzle

Another kind of question that has gained popularity in the Microsoft exams is "What Is The Result?" In this story problem, you're presented with an action that's been completed. The question stem gives you the action and you're supposed to pick the appropriate result of the action. The question is multiple choice — with a twist. Consider this example:

5 You configure a workgroup of Windows 98 computers to use TCP/IP automatic addressing. Using this configuration, the computers function normally by using TCP/IP. Six months later, you decide to add a DHCP server. What effect does this action have on the Windows 98 computers that use automatic IP addressing?

A ○ The Windows 98 computers must be configured to use the DHCP server and will not function until they are reconfigured.

B ○ The Windows 98 computers will function as long as there are no IP address conflicts with the DHCP server.

C ○ The Windows 98 computers will function if the DHCP server uses their preconfigured IP addresses for leasing purposes.

D ○ The Windows 98 computers will automatically use the DHCP server with no conflicts and without intervention from the administrator.

In this example, the correct answer is D. The question stem presents you with a completed "action," and your mission is to choose the correct "result" of that action.

Using your mouse for interface questions

Some of the certification exams now have interface questions. An interface question shows you some portion of the operating system's interface and asks you to click the part of the interface that would accomplish the required task. The question usually asks which options to select within the interface and tells you how many to choose. You then look at the interface screen, and using your mouse, click those areas. Consider this example:

6 You want your Windows NT Server to communicate over the Internet using the most secure form of authentication. In the Network Configuration window, which option should you select? (Click one selection.)

Along with this question, the exam interface displays the dialog box shown in Figure 8-1. To answer this question, you simply click the correct option in the sample dialog box that's displayed. For this example, the correct answer is Require Microsoft Encrypted Authentication, as shown in Figure 8-2.

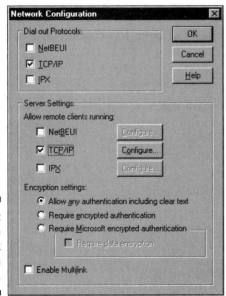

Figure 8-1:
The
Network
Configuration
window.

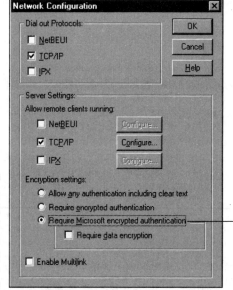

———The exam is looking for this response.

Figure 8-2:
The correct
answer to
this
interface
question.

Surviving scenario-based questions

You can expect to encounter a scenario-based question sometime in your
certification journey. The reputation for this kind of format is not particularly complimentary; the questions are generally very difficult and time-
consuming, making them the most disliked among test-takers. The question
presents you with a problem or scenario, plus the desired result and optional results. A proposed solution is also offered. The answer choices ask
you to determine whether the solution meets the required and optional
results, and you may see any number of possible combinations presented.
Consider this example:

7 Acme Gift Company needs to communicate with a new, small office
in San Diego from its Dallas office. To save connectivity charges, the
company would like to use a multilink connection for its Windows NT
computers.

Desired Result: Use a multilink connection to trade daily files and
information.

Optional Desired Results: Reduce administrative overhead and
provide a consistently reliable multilink connection.

Proposed Solution: Bind three 56K modems together at each site
and connect using an Internet Service Provider.

A ○ The proposed solution meets the required result and both of the optional results.

B ○ The proposed solution meets the required result and one of the optional results.

C ○ The proposed solution meets only the required result.

D ○ The proposed solution does not meet the required result.

As you can imagine, these questions tend to be quite complex and detailed. In this question, the correct answer is D, because multilink will not function properly using an Internet Service Provider.

Scenario questions require careful analysis on your part and can devour a lot of your time. However, you can develop tactics for managing these attention hogs; check out the next section for a few tips.

Working the Exam Questions to Weed Out the Right Answer

Now that you're familiar with your cast of test questions, we're here to tell you that you don't have to march into exam battle completely unarmed. Tactics exist to help you face even the toughest exam challenges. After all, we know that no matter how much you study and how much experience you have, you're never immune to the plague of an exam question or two that you just can't answer with complete confidence.

This is where the game of odds begins. The more things you can do to increase your odds of answering the question correctly, the better your odds of passing the exam. If you can increase your odds over and over during the exam, you are less likely to get a failing score. So how do you increase your odds? The answer is in knowing how to "work" the different kinds of exam questions.

Many new test-takers do themselves a great disservice by not logically examining the questions. The test becomes like a treasure hunt — the endless search for the hidden treasure rather than an exercise in logic. And at its core, the exam is a game of logic.

Scenario question panic mode

You may see two or three scenario questions in a row — enough to cause even the steadiest of test-takers to slip into a time panic. You can avoid this alarm by understanding that no exam is made up primarily of scenario questions. Focus on the question at hand while keeping a careful eye on your time limit.

If you know how to play the game and how to logically work the questions, you greatly increase your odds of passing the first time.

In addition to examining how to logically work the exam questions, the following sections present tactics for increasing your "odds" on any roll of the certification dice.

Responding when you know the answer

When you read a question and you absolutely know the answer . . . wait! Don't answer the question yet! The exam expects you to give the "best" answer for every question. New test-takers often make the mistake of answering questions they "know" too quickly. Although answer A may appear to be the correct answer, answer D may be a "better" answer. So the moral of this story is to read all the answer choices before you choose one.

The "best" answer is always going to be the right answer.

Handling questions you don't know

The bulk of our advice on handling the exam questions centers around questions you do not know or are not certain of. This is where your logic skills become critical as you try to find the correct answer. The following sections show you how to logically tackle the various exam questions we introduce earlier in this chapter.

Tackling multiple choice questions

This section covers a logical approach for simple multiple choice, Choose All That Apply questions, and Choose Three questions. These types of questions all work the same way, so we talk about them as a group.

In general, if you don't know the answer to a simple multiple choice question, you have to make a selection — a guess — which gives you a 25 percent chance of getting the question right because you usually find four options. But what if you could increase your odds? Well, you can! Here's what you do.

When taking an exam, if we hit questions that we just don't know or are not certain of the answer, we always work "in reverse." Instead of looking for the right answer, we look for what is not correct. Consider this example:

8 You want your Windows NT Server to dynamically resolve NetBIOS names to IP addresses/ What service can you use to accomplish this?

A ○ IPX/SPX

B ○ WINS

C ○ DHCP

D ○ IP Name Service

Assume that you don't know the answer to this question. If you don't know the answer, try to rule out what is not correct first. Often, if you look at the exam question this way, you can rule out at least two of the choices.

IPX/SPX is Novell's proprietary protocol, and you've never heard of the IP Name Service, so you rule those two out. Now you're left with answers B and C — WINS or DHCP. Instead of 25 percent odds, you now have a 50/50 chance of getting the correct answer. If you can increase your odds on every question you don't know, you're probably going to get some of them right, which may make all the difference when it comes time to tabulate your score. The correct answer, by the way, is WINS.

With Choose All That Apply questions, perform the same trick. First, try to rule out any answers that you know are incorrect. Your odds are not as good with this kind of question, because you have several possible combinations, but you can still increase your chances by working "in reverse."

For Choose Three, do the same thing. Rule out what is not correct. Because three of the answers are correct, if you can at least rule out two of the answer choices, you have only five left. (Remember, you usually have seven choices for this kind of question.) This process of elimination increases your chances of answering correctly.

For multiple choice questions and "multiple" multiple choice questions, work in reverse — rule out what is not correct first, then look for the correct answer(s).

Fall in love with scratch paper

If you take an entire exam and wind up with blank scratch paper, you can feel sure that you missed a great opportunity. Test-takers who use their scratch paper to jot down notes and draw diagrams for themselves perform better on the Microsoft exams than those who do not use the scratch paper.

Handling What Is The Result questions

With a "What is the result" question, you are presented with an action that has been taken and you are to pick the correct "result" for that action. Basically, these questions are still simple multiple choice questions — you just have to look at them a little differently.

The problem with these questions is the "confusion factor." Usually, the question gives you a lot of information, including stuff you don't need to know, just to try to confuse you. Often, the answer choices are complicated and similar to one another. The trick for this kind of question is to read the question, then try to answer the question without looking at the answer choices. Read the question, stop and think about the question, try to determine what the likely result will be, then look at the answer choices and see if your answer matches the exam answer.

In a sense, you're still trying to "rule out" other answer choices by first determining a probable answer. Even if your thoughts are incorrect, this step usually puts you on the right track for the correct answer. If you read the answer choices first, you may become confused — even if you really do know the answer.

Managing scenario-based questions

Scenario-based questions are the most difficult and time-consuming. You have a lot to read and you must go through several thought processes to come up with the correct answer.

Even scenario-based questions can't escape a few tricks that can save you time and help you find the right response. This is where your scratch paper comes in handy. The best approach is to read the scenario and take a few notes. By recording important details, you can refer to your notes instead of having to wade through the question again. Many test-takers hate to take notes because of the time involved, but in reality, notetaking on scenario-based questions actually saves you time.

Consider this example question:

9 Your company currently does not have a fault tolerant strategy for its Windows NT Servers. You would like to implement an effective fault tolerant strategy.

Required Result: You must be able to recover from a single disk failure.

Optional Desired Results: The strategy should not require excessive administrative overhead, and the strategy should not waste excessive amounts of disk space.

Proposed Solution: Implement disk mirroring on all Windows NT servers.

A ○ The proposed solution meets the required result and both of the optional results.

B ○ The proposed solution meets the required result and one of the optional results.

C ○ The proposed solution meets the required result only.

D ○ The proposed solution does not meet the required result.

Okay, here we go. The first thing you need to do is read the question stem and take notes as you go. Keep your notes very short. You can then refer to them as you logically tackle the question. Your notes on this question may look something like this:

> NT Servers need fault tolerant solution.
>
> R = Single disk failure recovery
>
> O = 1. Reduce admin time. 2. Not waste disk space
>
> S = Use disk mirroring

As you can see, the question now appears as a few lines that can refresh your memory on the goal and the required result, optional results, and the proposed solution. The information, in such a simple format, can help you determine the answer to the question.

The first thing you do is look at the required result and the solution. Does disk mirroring provide a fault tolerant solution for a single disk recovery? Yes, it does. So, if you look at the answer choices again, you can eliminate answer D:

A ○ The proposed solution meets the required result and both of the optional results.

B ○ The proposed solution meets the required result and one of the optional results.

C ○ The proposed solution meets the required result only.

D̶ ⊖ T̶h̶e̶ ̶p̶r̶o̶p̶o̶s̶e̶d̶ ̶s̶o̶l̶u̶t̶i̶o̶n̶ ̶d̶o̶e̶s̶ ̶n̶o̶t̶ ̶m̶e̶e̶t̶ ̶t̶h̶e̶ ̶r̶e̶q̶u̶i̶r̶e̶d̶ ̶r̶e̶s̶u̶l̶t̶.̶

Now only A, B, and C are left for your choosing. Next, look at the optional desired results. First, does disk mirroring reduce administrative overhead? The answer is yes. Disk mirroring is performed through a simple graphical user interface, and in the event of a disk failure, the disk mirror can become the actual disk in only a few moments through the GUI. So, you now know that the proposed solution meets the required result and at least one optional result: You can now rule out choice C:

A ○ The proposed solution meets the required result and both of the optional results.

B ○ The proposed solution meets the required result and one of the optional results.

~~C ⊖ The proposed solution meets the required result only.~~

~~D ⊖ The proposed solution does not meet the required result.~~

Do you notice what's happening? By logically looking at the question, you can start from the bottom of the list and work your way backward, eliminating the choices as you go.

The next step is to look at the next optional desired result. Does disk mirroring reduce the waste to disk space? The answer is no. Disk mirroring basically makes a copy of the disk, so any mirrored disk requires two disks. Disk mirroring wastes the most amount of disk space compared to other fault tolerant methods, so this desired optional result is not met. Therefore, the correct answer to the question is B.

The only way to answer scenario questions correctly is to use a logical approach to the question. If you simply read the question and try to pick the correct answer, the odds of you getting the question right are small. Use your scratch paper and logically analyze the question!

Chapter 9

On the Day of the Exam

. . . .

In This Chapter

▶ Getting off to a good start

▶ Taming your nervousness

▶ Exploring the exam center process

. . . .

*T*he day finally dawns for you to deliver your saturated brain to the moment of truth: THE CERTIFICATION EXAM. You may awake on this morning with a deep sense of dread, a feeling of panic, or perhaps even with calm assurance. Whatever your state of mind, you need to take a few steps on exam day to stay focused and ready to tackle the ultimate test.

Following a Pre-Test Routine

The day of the exam tends be a strange animal. The stress the exam places on test-takers often causes behavior that's negative to the testing experience. The good news is that the more exams you take, the better you're able to manage your routine and avoid doing things that can harm your ability to test well. You can steer clear of these negative behaviors and give yourself the edge you need by remembering these important points:

✔ The test day is not a study day. You can spend a little time reviewing for your exam, but we caution you not to try to learn new content at this late date.

✔ Avoid doing anything that's outside your typical daily schedule. The day of your exam is not the best time to take up jogging.

✔ Keep your normal eating schedule. If you have a morning exam, make sure that you eat breakfast if that meal is a part of your normal routine. If you have a 1 p.m. exam, enjoy a light lunch before you take the test.

✔ Avoid scheduling your exam on a day when you have other major activities taking place. For example, if you have a major presentation to some business clients, don't try to tackle the exam on the same day. Choose a day that's as stress-free as possible — except for the exam!

✔ Allow plenty of time to relax and make your way to the testing center. Plan to do nothing but focus on the upcoming exam experience for at least two hours before heading out for your test.

Avoiding the Cramming Syndrome

The Cramming Syndrome — those acts of taking in large gulps of last-minute study out of sheer desperation — can tempt even the toughest of certification customers. Although this alarm mode may seem appropriate for a technical exam, research shows over and over that candidates who cram before an exam do not perform as well as those who avoid cramming.

We need to define the difference between "cramming" and "reviewing." You can review your notes on the day of the exam. This last look serves as a systematic, final pass over your notes and material. Cramming is a frenzied approach to scanning your notes over and over. Some test-takers continue to gallop through their study materials until only a few moments before they take the exam. The result? You stride in to take the exam with a frazzled mind. When you begin the exam questions, which are designed to test your knowledge of small details, you become confused, tired, and prone to another panic attack.

The best way to review your notes is to read through them completely one time. Then, put your notes away, promising yourself to not look at any content during the hour before your exam. If you write a cheat sheet before you take the exam, you can plan to review that information for about ten minutes before you take the exam. We cover developing a cheat sheet for yourself in detail in Chapter 6.

Managing Stress

Certification carries the sound of the "S" word we all know too well — stress. Many new test-takers underestimate how stressful exam day can be. After all, it's just a test, right? Well, the reality is that you've spent a lot of time studying for your MCSE exams and no doubt, a substantial amount of money. The exam itself is a $100 investment.

Managing the stress of the day can make a difference in your performance on the exam. You can tackle the tension in a couple of ways. First, pick a day for your exam that's not overcrowded and stressful. You need the day to focus on the exam without a lot of other distractions. Try to stay relaxed on the day of the exam — don't try to tackle other problems or issues you face. Wear your favorite clothes to take your exam — dress comfortably.

Donuts, anyone?

Stay away from sugar-loaded breakfast foods, such as donuts, or heavy lunch and dinner meals before your exam. These kinds of foods, although a joy to eat, will slow your brain down — hardly what you're hoping for on the day of the exam. Also, avoid excessive caffeine consumption. You don't want to "bottom out" during the exam.

To help rein in your racing thoughts, plan to arrive at the testing center a half-hour early. Before you go into the center, give yourself a few minutes just to sit in your car and relax. Listen to some music, get mentally ready, or just relax — but don't start cramming for the exam.

During the exam, if you begin to feel anxious, give yourself a "30-second vacation." Close your eyes, breathe deeply, and imagine yourself in a place that relaxes you — the beach, the mountains, the freeway — wherever! This short visualization exercise can get your nerves in check and help you to refocus your efforts on the exam.

Finally, pause to remind yourself that the test is not a matter of life and death. Although you want to pass on the first try, the world is not likely to end if you miss the mark — you can always retake the test. Try to keep everything in proper perspective.

Stress is a normal part of the testing process. Expect to be nervous before the exam — most test-takers experience at least a few jitters when they're called upon to show what they know.

Knowing What to Expect at the Exam Center

The process at the testing center is rather simple. Of course, you're not allowed to take any of your notes or paper into the exam center. You can bring a pen or pencil, or you can borrow one from the exam proctors.

Avoiding panic

Some people get so nervous during the exam that they begin to feel sick. You can help avoid this feeling by eating a healthy and light meal before you take the exam. A little nourishment usually has a calming effect that can ward off panic. Also, if you begin feeling too nervous during the exam, stop, close your eyes, breathe deeply, and count to ten. You're likely to feel refreshed and refocused.

When you arrive, you need to check in with the test administrator. Expect to provide two forms of identification, one of which must be a picture ID (your Social Security card and driver's license are good choices). After you sign in, the test administrator will ask you how many sheets of scratch paper you want. For safe measure, request three sheets. Unfortunately, you can't keep the notes you make during the exam — you have to return the scratch paper to the test administrator after your exam. The test administrator also hands over a form that explains the rules of the testing center. After you read the form, you're required to sign it.

The exams are completely closed-book, which means no notes, laptops, handheld computers, or any data storage device. Pagers and cell phones are also contraband in the testing center. Basically, it's up to you, your brain, your pencil, and the computer the center provides.

After you check in, you may have to wait a few minutes before you can go into the testing center. Look at this slight delay as a great opportunity to pace the floor and wring your hands.

Every testing center is different, but you can expect to see a room with 5 to 15 computers. The computers function just like PCs, but the testing software has control of the system for security purposes. The room may have a window so that the proctor can watch candidates, or it may even have a video camera for security — just don't make faces at it.

Once inside the testing center, you hear an explanation of how the exam works, and then you're ready to begin your test. If you have questions, make sure that you ask them before the exam begins.

Enjoying the Calm Before the Test Storm

Now that you're sitting in front of the computer, you have the opportunity to breathe deeply before you type in your name and Social Security number, which signals the beginning of the exam. Take about five minutes to create your cheat sheet on your scratch paper.

Don't be late!

Because many people use the test center's computers on any given day — and someone may be waiting in the wings to enjoy his or her own moment of exam fame — you can't be late for your exam. If you are late, you may not be able to take the test and you can't expect to receive a refund because of your tardiness. Allow yourself plenty of time to arrive at the testing center.

The test administrator may penalize you on your time if you hesitate too long to actually begin the exam. Write out your notes, and then get rolling.

With your braindump done, you can take a few minutes to try a test demonstration that is available. This demo helps you get used to the testing software so that you don't run into any surprises during the exam. After you complete the demo and answer the survey, begin the exam. You've arrived at the moment when all your work and study can truly shine. Remind yourself to think carefully and positively, remain calm, and go for it!

You have to turn in your notes at the end of the exam. Test administrators look harshly on anyone who considers hanging on to even a shred of exam-related information.

Answering the Big Question: Did I Pass?

Did you pass the exam? If you did, congratulations! You are now ready to move on with your MCSE studies — oh joy, the next exam. If not, then give yourself time to regroup and prepare to take the test again. Chapter 10 gives you specific instructions for retaking the test — just a stopover on the road to certification success.

Can I take a break?

You can take a break during the exam, if necessary. The administrator will note your break and ask you to sign in and sign out. Be advised, however, that your exam time doesn't pause when you, for example, visit the restroom. For a regular 90-minute exam, we suggest that you avoid taking a break if at all possible.

Chapter 10

What to Do If You Don't Pass the First Time

So you click the End Exam button and you see a red failing line. You did not pass the exam on the first try. Failing an exam is frustrating, to say the least, but we assure you that a no-pass is not at all unusual. In fact, very few MCSEs make it through the entire certification process without having to retake some of the exams. Congratulations! You're normal!

That little pep talk doesn't change the fact that you have to retake the exam, and after a failure, many people find themselves staring at a pile of notes and not knowing what to do. Don't worry, this chapter shows you how to regroup and get ready to take the test again.

Performing a Braindump

We bring up the word *braindump* a few times in this book. Sounds a little gross, but a braindump means that you simply write down everything you can remember about the exam on a piece of paper — ideally, as soon after you leave the test center as possible. Unfortunately, candidates sometimes become so upset when they fail an exam that they storm out of the exam location and take hours (or days) to get over the trauma.

This common, normal action of becoming agitated, however, can only contribute to you failing the exam a second time. Now, we know that that prediction seems like a strong statement — after all, you deserve to be upset, right? Well, maybe, but giving in to an emotional response is not wise, and here's why.

This time right after the exam, even though you did not pass, presents a golden opportunity. Your brain has a lot of the test still stored in its temporary memory. You may not remember specific questions, but you can recall concepts and questions that you had particular problems with. Don't expect this information-rich time to last long. In a few hours, those test specifics you have implanted in your head will become fuzzy and distorted. In a day or so, only the basics will remain clear.

Because the first few minutes after the exam are so packed with power and potential, we suggest that you follow this course of action:

1. **Check out at the testing center, take your score report, and go immediately to your car.**

2. **Get a piece of paper and a pencil, and do a braindump — write down everything you can remember.**

Be as specific as possible. You don't have to try to repeat questions to yourself, but you can write down things like, "seven or eight questions on user profiles, several RAS questions, and security," and other similar phrases. If you can remember specific questions you had trouble with, write them down.

After you create your braindump, you have a terrifically valuable piece of paper to help you regroup and study for your exam. Can you expect the same exam next time? No. But now you have a very good idea about what the exam likes to focus on!

Analyzing Your Score Report

The score report can give you clues about your weak areas, but be sure to place the information in proper context. On your score report, you will see the exam's six focal categories and a percentage score that shows how well you performed in each category. The reports look something like this:

- ✔ Planning — 10%
- ✔ Installation and Configuration — 75%
- ✔ Managing Resources — 88%
- ✔ Connectivity — 66%
- ✔ Monitoring and Optimization — 20%
- ✔ Troubleshooting — 10%

Preparing for a braindump

A good action to take before you end the exam is to spend a few minutes scanning through the test, mentally noting the kinds of questions you had trouble answering. This way, you're preparing to do a braindump if you do not pass. Although you may find it hard to make yourself focus on the possibility of a no-pass, you may later thank yourself for the forethought.

The problem with the score report is that the percentages don't mean a lot because you don't know how many questions are in each category. For example, Troubleshooting — 10%. Does that mean you missed nine out of ten questions or what? The fact is, you don't really know, unless you tried to keep count as you took the test.

A serious mistake is to focus your studies only on the categories in which you performed poorly. Yes, pay attention to those, but note the other categories as well. Do not start thinking, "If I can just nail troubleshooting next time, I will pass." So, use the score report to give you some guidance, but don't become obsessed with it!

Another piece of information the score report can give you is, well, your score! If the exam required you to make a 590 to pass and you made a 575, you only missed a question or two — actually, a dreadful thought. You can regroup and focus on your weak areas and your braindump with confidence that you'll probably pass the second time. If the exam required you to score 590 to pass and you made a 320, then you need to spend time restudying the book and your notes — you're not scoring close enough to the mark and are missing way too many questions.

My score was really low

If your score was really low, don't give up. Use your braindump and your score report to guide you, but consider taking one of the practice exams just to see what areas are difficult for you. Try to pinpoint specific topics, then reread those sections of the book. You probably need to take additional notes and completely regroup all the information to get on track. But you can do it — others can attest to their success the second time around!

Regrouping with Your Notes

Your score was reasonably close to passing, and you now have your braindump and your score report to serve your regrouping efforts. The next step is pay a visit to your notes. Say that you took the NT Server exam and the Performance Monitor questions really got you. You didn't study Performance Monitor a lot, and you just didn't know the answers to those questions. Go though your notes and highlight any information you have on Performance Monitor, then go through your *MCSE ...For Dummies* book and read the Performance Monitor section again. Can you add new notes about Performance Monitor after rereading? Probably so.

Perform this same action with any other areas in which you felt weak. Use your braindump and your score report to guide you.

Try to focus on the details. Use your braindump to try to recall specific issues. For example, did the Performance Monitor questions focus on configuring counters or what services it can provide? Try to remember the details and focus your study on those details.

Studying . . . Again

After you regroup with your notes, you're likely to have some additional material to study. Your new notes focus on your weak areas, so they pull out all kinds of extra details you need for the exam.

Use the same study process of memorizing your notes, using flash cards, and employing the other study skills you developed over the course of your initial test preparation. Chapter 5 gives you a number of study tips and tactics to use.

More notes, anyone?

As much as you hate the idea, consider starting a new page of notes. Focus these fresh notes on the topics from your braindump and what you determine to be your weak areas from your score report. This rewriting and gathering of additional information can increase your knowledge of that content.

I don't have a computer!

If you don't have access to a computer at home, you can pursue a few other options. If your business has computers, find out if you can use one for practice purposes. Companies that are supportive of your studies are usually eager to find ways to support your efforts. Also, many county libraries now have rather advanced computer labs. And check out community colleges or even nearby universities. Many colleges allow you to pay a fee to use the computer lab, even if you're not a student.

Practicing on Your Computer

If you have a computer available, take the time to practice your newfound skills. Translating a textbook description to a real working experience is the best way to remember a process. Use your NT Server to practice setting up Performance Monitor counters, climb through the RAS interface, and figure out how to configure it. This hands-on practice makes a world of difference.

Hands-on practice usually reduces study time because you have reinforcement for what you see on a printed page. Your notes actually come to life, giving you a well-rounded look at the exam content and why the Microsoft folks think it's important.

Motivating Yourself

After failing an exam, some certification candidates experience what we call the "stop factor." You come back to the table, begin restudying, then you just want to quit. This sensation is quite normal; the frustration is often caused by pushing yourself too hard. Trying to study when you're not motivated is a losing battle. So how to you get back onboard? Here are two tips:

- ✔ Take a break. Give yourself a weekend to do some things you put off — especially the fun stuff. Don't touch a computer and don't look at your book or your notes. At a certain saturation point, your brain simply needs a break. Grant yourself this break and let your brain rest. Rather than being a waste of time, this hiatus is time well-spent.

- ✔ Need some additional motivation? Check out Chapters 14, 15, and 16. These chapters focus on finding and securing an MCSE position! You can cruise some Web sites and see what's available out there (including the pay!). Job shopping is a great way to remind yourself of your goals while re-energizing for another round of test-taking.

Assessing Your Progress

After you refocus, study, and hopefully have an opportunity to practice, you're ready to wade through the assessment exams again. Use every assessment exercise you have in your *MCSE ...For Dummies* book, including the short exercises at the end of each chapter, and the full length practice exams in the appendix and on the CD-ROM. Additionally, try to use third-party practice exams, such as those available from Transcender. Information and samples from third-party exams are available on the CD-ROM that comes with all *MCSE ...For Dummies* books. Answer the questions on the practice exams, study the responses, and even try to explain why incorrect answer choices are incorrect.

You may need to use these assessment exercises and exams several times. Make sure that you consistently score well on all the assessment exercises before you attempt to tackle the real exam a second time.

Don't forget to use the assessment exams to add information to your notes. Pay careful attention to questions that focus on content that you had trouble with the first time. You're likely to see additional details that you can add to your notes.

Giving the Exam Another Shot

Okay, so you regrouped, you restudied, you're jamming on the practice exams, and now you're confident that you can try the test again. You need to call Sylvan Prometric or Virtual University Enterprises (VUE) to schedule the exam again (and pay again as well). After you complete your registration, plan out your schedule so that you have plenty of time to focus when exam day arrives.

You may feel some extra nervousness the second time around — a normal response to the challenge before you. Try to keep your mind focused on the exam, concentrate on what you've learned, remember how to tackle the exam questions with logical thinking, and don't forget to work carefully.

You will pass the exam! Scoring well may take some time, and it may take additional work, but the people who are successful with MCSE certification exams are those who are tenacious and do not give up! You can often learn as much or more from your mistakes, so take this opportunity to learn!

Web help

Don't forget to check out Internet sites to help you as you restudy for the exam. These sites may be able to give you additional study tips and hints about facing the exam — the first or subsequent times.

Part IV
The Part of Tens

In this part . . .

Ah, The Part of Tens. This is the place to go if you want to add to your already amazing repertoire of MCSE information and insight. Chapters in this part sweep the gamut of certification topics — from abbreviations you must remember to study tips you can't forget. You also find friendly advice about tracking down just the right job, using the Internet to show off your credentials, and asking critical questions when you're being interviewed by a potential employer — all this and a cartoon, too!

Chapter 11

Ten MCSE Abbreviations You Can't Live Without

*W*e all know how much Microsoft loves abbreviations and acronyms. You probably already figured out how often these linked letters come into play during certification study. But you also can expect to hear some important abbreviations tossed into talk of the MCSE designation as well. Here are ten commonly mentioned sets of initials that you may hear around the industry — you can throw them out at parties to make yourself look highly intelligent.

AATP — Authorized Academic Training Partner

The initials AATP identify an institution that's authorized by Microsoft to teach Microsoft curriculum. Most all AATPs are academic institutions, including junior colleges, high schools, colleges, and universities. The certification courses are taught according to the institution's school calendar rather than the fast-paced, intensive schedule of an Authorized Technical Education Center (ATEC).

AATPs are similar to ATECs. However, AATPs are not required to use the Microsoft Official Curriculum (MOC). Also, an AATP does not require Microsoft Certified Trainers (MCTs) to teach the courses.

AATPs are part of the Microsoft initiative to provide certification training in high schools and colleges. It's much easier for an organization to qualify for AATP status than ATEC (and much less expensive).

ATEC — Authorized Technical Education Center

Microsoft authorizes ATECs to teach certification studies using the Microsoft Official Curriculum (MOC). All instructors must be Microsoft Certified Trainers (MCTs).

MCP — Microsoft Certified Professional

You can earn MCP certification by passing any Microsoft exam *except* Networking Essentials.

MCSD — Microsoft Certified Solution Developer

Any individual who passes four specific Microsoft exams earns the MCSD certification, which attests to a high level of expertise in the arena of computer program development, specifically with Microsoft BackOffice products.

MCSE — Microsoft Certified Systems Engineer

Any individual who passes six specific Microsoft exams earns MCSE certification. This designation communicates a high level of expertise in the arena of computer networking, specifically with Microsoft Windows NT products.

MCSE+Internet

This add-on certification indicates a high level of competence in Internet technologies. The MCSE+Internet certification consists of the basic MCSE plus three to five additional exams such as TCP/IP, Proxy Server 2, and Internet Explorer Administration Kit.

MCT — Microsoft Certified Trainer

Any individual who achieves MCP, MCSE, or MCSD status, as well as demonstrating skills or specific training in instruction methods, earns the MCT certification. An MCT is authorized to train students at ATECs and other Microsoft approved and non-approved sites. You can find specific requirements for the MCT at `www.microsoft.com/mct`.

MOC — Microsoft Official Curriculum

MOC is the Microsoft "official" courseware taught by Microsoft Certified Trainers (MCTs) in Authorized Technical Education Centers (ATECs).

MSDN — Microsoft Developer Network

The developer network includes the free online Microsoft Knowledge Base as well as subscriptions to a variety of services, including the massive library of information on all Microsoft products.

MSP — Microsoft Solution Provider

MSPs consult with clients, in conjunction with Microsoft, to integrate Microsoft products into the workplace. Authorized Technical Education Centers (ATECs) can also be MSPs, providing training to third-party organizations.

Chapter 12
Ten MCSE Study Tips You Must Not Forget

In This Chapter

▶ Zeroing in on proper planning with the exam preparation guides

▶ Pulling out and highlighting details

▶ Taking study one chapter at a time

▶ Using tools to train your memory

S tudy, study, study. That's what the certification process is really all about. This chapter pulls out the study tips that we feel most strongly about from previous chapters. Use this chapter as a quick reference guide to effectively studying your way to MCSE certification!

Planning Your Study and Training

First and foremost, if you don't take the time and initiative to plan, you're wasting every other tip in this book, and you can expect to be very disappointed. But more importantly, you're missing techniques that can enable you to succeed on your exams and in your career.

Relying on the Exam Preparation Guides

The Microsoft exam preparation guides provide a tried and true means to plan your studies. Remember, Microsoft prepares these exams. So it makes sense that if the guides suggest that X or Y is on the exam, then you need to study X and Y. For the same reason, TechNet is a rich study resource. After all, Microsoft uses TechNet as a major reference for exam preparation, so you're wise to tap into TechNet, too.

Sweating the Details

The exam focuses on small details. Stay alert to those details as you study. Although you need to understand the broad concepts and functions of various system components, the true test of your comprehension is in the minor points that can surface as major obstacles to exam success. For example, where are user profiles stored by default? This level of technical detail is critical to your study plan.

Staying Clear of Highlighter Heaven

The highlighter is your friend, but don't buddy up so much that you mark every line in your *MCSE ...For Dummies* book from cover to cover! Highlight important details and phrases, but be careful of including too much information. Use highlighted passages to guide your notetaking and to help you focus on the specifics.

Compiling Chapter Notes

Be sure to take notes as you work through your *MCSE ...For Dummies* book — chapter by chapter. Use your highlighter to help you focus on the details and technical content for your notes, then write down that chapter's content in an organized manner before moving to the next chapter. Packaging your studies by chapter really helps. We promise!

Studying as You Go

Okay, you take notes in a systematic, chapter-by-chapter manner. Then what? As you work through each chapter of your *MCSE ...For Dummies* book, stop and study. You don't want to wait until you finish your book to try to learn everything. You can successfully manage the content if you study the material along the way. This way, you can memorize content over a period of weeks instead of all at once. Also, figuring out the content as you go can make later chapters easier to understand and master.

Remembering to Memorize

You can't find an easy way around it — you absolutely must memorize technical content, abbreviations, and acronyms. First, you have to understand your learning style, then you need to select the memorization methods that work for you. Rewriting, audio- and videotapes, mnemonics, and a variety of other tactics are available to help you commit important details to memory.

Making Flash Cards

Flash cards are a great training tool, especially if you make them yourself. Learning content "out of order" reinforces memory, and the cards are portable — you can carry them around with you to review when you have a few spare moments. Also, use your flash cards to practice "system sequence" processes. For example, as you study for the NT exams, use flash cards to practice repeating the NT boot sequence.

Creating a Cheat Sheet

Do yourself a favor: Create a cheat sheet — in your brain! Distill your notes down to one page of highly important information, and then memorize that page. To be fully prepared for the exam, practice rewriting the page without checking your notes. Then, right before you begin your test at the exam center, re-create your cheat sheet on your scratch paper so that you can use it during the test. This tactic is very helpful — and perfectly legal at the testing center!

Using Assessment Tools

Assessment exercises and practice exams can save your life! Use them to check your progress and to discover areas where you are weak and need more study. You can also add to your notes by picking up details from assessment tools. The *Certification ...For Dummies* series supports your efforts by providing a variety of practice exams in each of its titles — all designed to acquaint you with exam format before you face the real deal on test day.

Chapter 13

Ten MCSE Study and Testing Pitfalls to Avoid

*N*o doubt, we often learn best from our mistakes. But if we can avoid those mistakes, we often save a lot of time. This chapter tells you about ten MCSE study and testing pitfalls you must avoid. These pitfalls can slow you down and pull your testing off track — watch out for them!

I'll Study after I Read the Book

Many a new MCSE candidate can attest to the fateful foolishness of this move. Preparing for certification exams is not like studying for other tests. Because the MCSE exams are riddled with highly technical content, you study each chapter as you progress through your *MCSE ...For Dummies* book. If you wait until you finish the book, you're likely to fall victim to the overwhelming load of details and acronyms. If you study as you go, you can make sense of the technical content in small bites, making each subject easier to digest.

I Can Highlight without Taking Notes

Hmm, here's a bad habit left over from high school or college days. So you think you can read the book, highlight important information, and then review your highlighted material without taking notes? Although a few people may succeed with this approach, most of us can perform much better on the exam if we convert the highlighted information into notes for our systematic study.

As Long As I Get the Big Picture, I'll Do Fine

The exam focuses on the little stuff. Studying small details can make or break your performance. Yes, you do need to understand the "big picture," but major concepts won't provide enough information for a passing score. MCSEs are expected to know the intricacies of operating systems and network design — the exam tests your knowledge of the details.

The Exam Questions Are Bound to Be Straightforward

The exam questions are difficult and often very confusing. Many MCSE candidates trust that the exams are always straightforward — in other words, if you know the content fairly well, you can pick out the correct answer. Call that notion wishful thinking. You must know details and understand the content in order to determine logically the correct answers to the questions.

I Can Trust Information I Find on the Internet

The Internet is packed with information about the MCSE exams, but Microsoft doesn't endorse these sites. Much of what you may find is questionable at best, so be forewarned. Make a practice of using Microsoft-approved study materials to be sure that your information is accurate and up-to-date.

I Won't Be Stressed on the Exam Day

Many candidates underestimate the amount of stress the exam can inspire. The sudden nervousness catches candidates off guard and often causes negative behaviors, such as cramming. If you understand that the exam is likely to cause you stress, you can prepare to deal with it appropriately.

I Should Mark Every Question I'm Uncertain Of

A fair share of new test-takers succumb to this common pitfall. Remember to mark only those questions that you have a reasonable chance of answering correctly with further review. Do not mark questions that you absolutely do not know. Your best choice is to make an educated guess on those questions, and then move on.

The Exam Is Timed, So I Have to Hurry

For most exams, you have more than enough time if you read at a normal rate. Many candidates become too concerned about the exam time. This concern causes them to work too quickly and make careless mistakes. Yes, watch your time, but don't waste your energy wondering whether you're going to run out.

If I Have Enough Time at the End of the Exam, I Should Review All the Questions

Rather than return to every question, trust your first instinct — that gut feeling is usually reliable. If you change an answer at the end of the exam, you accept a high risk of missing that question. By this time, you're tired and are likely to second-guess your answers. Try not to change any answer after you finish the exam, unless you're absolutely convinced you're making the right choice!

If I Need to Take an Exam Over, I Should Reschedule It for the Next Day

The exam-taking process is grueling — pass or fail. If you're in the latter category this time around, allow yourself a few days to regroup, study, revisit the practice exams, and prepare for the exam. Although you may want to quickly reschedule the exam and try it again, such haste is usually not a good idea. Give yourself some time; you're likely to enjoy the payoff on your next attempt.

Chapter 14

Ten Tips for Looking for an MCSE Job

*P*lay this one right and you can have employers eating out of your hand. But don't be cocky either. Your goal is to be a professional and prove your abilities as an MCSE.

Writing Your MCSE Resumé to Guarantee Inquiries

Keep the following points in mind when you prepare your resumé:

✔ Put your resumé on white paper in a neat — not handwritten — format. Don't use fancy graphics or fonts. Remember that most resumés are just scanned, not absorbed word for word.

✔ We don't believe resumé length is important as long as everything on the resumé is relevant. For most people, however, that's two pages, tops!

✔ Show performance in your resumé. Use specific numbers and accomplishments. Make sure that you list all MCSE exams that you've passed.

✔ Don't forget to include technical references. Include everything that's relevant, including on-the-job training, apprentice programs, and volunteer work.

✔ Keep your sentences short and focused. Verbose sentences and paragraphs with metaphors and adjectives are great for novels, but most employers just don't have the time to read all that stuff.

✔ List only information about yourself that is relevant to your job search.

✔ Include your name and contact information on each page. Don't forget to list your e-mail address and Web page, if you have one.

✔ Be consistent. Whatever order you choose to list information, follow the same pattern throughout the resumé.

✔ Ask for opinions! Make changes! Revise, revise, and revise! No one's ever invented a perfect resumé.

Researching the Company

Spend some time researching your prospective employer. The Internet is a great place to start. And if a lull occurs during the interview, you can make a good impression by saying something like, "When I was at your Web site, I noticed that sales for this latest quarter are higher than a year ago. What's driving that?"

Aside from the Internet, the best reference is from another employee. Try to obtain a reference from someone who already works at the company through directory listings and even through information you gain on the Internet.

Putting Together a Pre-Interview Checklist

Run down the following points when you're preparing for an interview:

✔ You need business cards. If you have a qualifying exam under your belt, have business cards printed with the MCP logo. Do this even if you're unemployed. Certification is very professional, and those letters carry a lot of weight among companies who consider the exams to be a demonstration of your expertise — and stamina.

✔ When you make the interview appointment, ask about the company's dress code for interviews. If you feel uncomfortable inquiring, then always go to an interview dressed in business formal attire. Keep in mind that most companies are casual on Fridays, and some businesses are casual all the time, but your best bet is to dress formally for an interview.

✔ Keep a portfolio of your certifications to show the prospective employer. It's also a good idea to devote a section of your resumé to your current certifications.

✔ Prepare questions before the interview. The interviewer will always ask you if you have any questions. You need to have at least a few so that you can demonstrate your interest and enthusiasm. We suggest ten good questions in Chapter 16.

✔ Practice the interview. Answering questions with ease demonstrates your communication skills.

✔ Prepare several folders (minimum three) containing your business card, resumé, personal and professional references, MCSE/MCP transcript, and other applicable documents. You're then all set if the employer doesn't have your resumé or if several people participate in the interview. You also prove your well-prepared nature!

✔ Make sure that you know how to find the interview location. If you need driving directions, go to www.mapquest.com for online door-to-door directions. If the route looks complicated, try the trip out the night before. No matter what you do, don't be late!

Carrying Important Stuff to Your Interview

Always carry the following items with you:

✔ Business cards

✔ Resumé

✔ A list of contacts within the interviewing company

Reviewing Your Job Interview Checklist

Keep the following points in mind as you head for the interview:

- ✔ Arrive ahead of the appointment time.

- ✔ Be flexible and cool. Prospective employers ask questions to purposefully make you sweat. If you flub up, laugh and move on. Your ability to demonstrate self-assurance is crucial.

- ✔ Be yourself. Your resumé is your ticket to the interview, but you are the show they have come to see. So don't pretend to be something you're not.

- ✔ Sit still during the interview. Keep both feet on the floor, legs together (you heard us right, legs together), hands folded in your lap. Look people in the eye when you speak with them, but don't conduct a staring contest.

- ✔ The company may want you to participate in a second interview on the spot. Whatever happens, "bend like a willow," or be flexible.

- ✔ Be prepared for a battery of technical questions. Hey, you may have to show what you know in a written test.

- ✔ Practice "active listening." Listen carefully to what the interviewer is saying and take notes. When the interviewer stops talking, paraphrase what he or she has said. For example, after the interviewer explains the job responsibilities to you, say something like, "So, my understanding is that the major responsibilities of this position are. . . . "

- ✔ Ask for the interviewer's business card. After the interview, send a thank-you note via either regular or e-mail.

Knowing What Questions to Expect

Write down your answers to the questions that you expect to hear — from research or personal experience — and anything else that you can anticipate. Then, rehearse them so that you can reply instantly. Whatever you do, do not *read* the answers to these practice questions. Talk off the top of your head — this is not a recitation.

Here are some likely candidates for interview questions:

- ✔ "What do you do when you see a Windows blue screen?" is an example of a hypothetical question. If you have to field this type of inquiry, try to think of a situation similar to the one you're being asked about. For example, you may respond to the blue-screen question with "Well, it's interesting that you should ask that. Just the other day, a computer on the system I work with had a blue screen and I. . . . "

✔ What is your greatest strength and your most pronounced weakness? Yep, they still ask these questions. Make sure your greatest strength is actually true. Don't say your greatest strength is rolling out complex NT implementations if you've never done that. Also, try to capitalize on your weakness and make sure it is job-related. You don't want to say, "Oh, I probably drink too much." You would want to say, "I have a tendency to work too hard." Whatever you say, be honest.

✔ Tell us about the worst problem you've ever had on the job. Do not, we repeat, do not say a single bad word about any person or company that you've worked for. The prospective employer sees this negativity as a clue about what you're inclined to say in your *next* job interview.

✔ What do you consider your greatest accomplishment?

✔ Why do you want this job?

✔ Why should we hire you?

✔ Where would you like to be in five years?

✔ Why are you leaving your current employer?

✔ Expect questions about your resumé. So be sure you know what's on it!

✔ Do you have any other questions? Ask questions and reserve the right to call the employer with other questions.

Negotiating a Terrific Salary

Never be the first to mention salary. However, be prepared to answer with a number. Know what you need to be happy and what you can settle for. If you're willing to bargain, offer a range. If benefits are important, ask about company benefits before you quote a salary.

Although conventional wisdom suggests letting the employer offer the salary figure, don't disregard the power of negotiation. In today's job market, you have the edge, and companies are usually willing to work with you on your expectations.

You can always answer an employer's question about salary with a question of your own: "What are you offering?" But don't play games with a prospective employer. If you are firm about a certain amount, ask yourself these questions: Can you comfortably accept less, are you inclined to stay with the company, and do you expect to be happy working for the organization? The answers are all up to you.

Holding Back an Immediate Response to Any Job Offer

No matter how much you want the job, never accept or decline a job during the interview. Ask the employer if you can "sleep on it." If they want you, they'll wait. A delayed response serves several purposes:

- ✔ You demonstrate that you don't make quick decisions about important issues.
- ✔ You're put in control of the interview.
- ✔ You can take time to think about this important decision.

Of course, a fine line exists between thinking things over and leaving a prospective employer hanging. It's all right to "sleep on it," as long as you don't sleep on it for a week. You should let the employer know something, or at least follow up with additional questions, within three days. In this way, you show a prospective employer that you're not only careful but also time-conscious and considerate.

Chapter 15

Ten Web Sites for Job Hunting and Posting Your Resumé

. . . .

In This Chapter

▶ Using online job search engines and online resumés
▶ Reviewing important technical job sites

. . . .

*T*he happy day finally arrives — you are an MCSE and you're ready to find a new job! Or, maybe the happy day hasn't arrived just yet, but you need a little motivation to support your continuing career search. This chapter identifies ten Web sites that can help you find a job, put you in touch with prospective employers or agencies, post your resumé online for the world to see, or at least remind you of your occupational goal.

All the sites we list in this chapter are free — you don't pay a fee to use the site and you don't get charged if you want to post your resumé on the site. Technical employees are in such great demand that companies often use these sites to search for employees both by advertising and through the resumés posted on the sites.

The sites are rather intuitive — you can search for any certain kind of technical job, usually by geographic location. Also, the site's main page typically has a link that enables you to post your resumé on the site. If you want to post your resumé, click the link and make sure you follow the online instructions completely. Most of these sites have resumé requirements and restrictions on the length of the resumé.

Finally, if you decide to post your resumé on these sites, consider getting a temporary e-mail address so that all the job queries you receive from interested companies come to one e-mail address dedicated for this purpose. You can get a free hotmail e-mail address from Microsoft at www.hotmail.com or a free Yahoo! e-mail account by clicking the corresponding link at www.yahoo.com.

You can also create your own "resumé home page" by using a Web development application such as FrontPage 98, and then posting it on a free Web page at www.geocities.com. This tactic enables you to completely customize your online resumé and shows employers that you are Internet savvy.

Online Career Center

The Online Career Center — OCC — enables you to perform specialized job searches by city, state, or field. This site, shown in Figure 15-1, focuses on technical careers and hosts a "personal career center" on online job fairs. Check it out at www.occ.com.

Computer Jobs

Computer Jobs, available at www.computerjobs.com, also enables you to perform customized job searches by city, state, and field. Like OCC, Computer Jobs is a dedicated resource for IT professionals. This site has numerous articles about IT professional jobs, and you can post your resumé on the site. Figure 15-2 shows the home page for Computer Jobs.

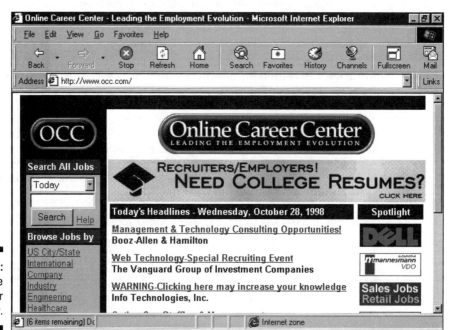

Figure 15-1: The Online Career Center.

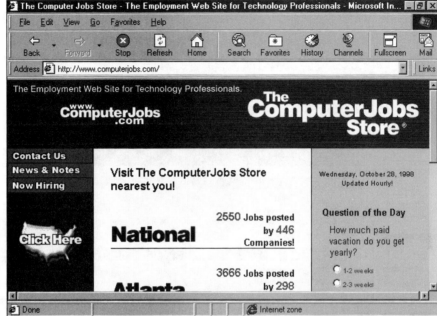

Figure 15-2:
The
Computer
Jobs Web
site.

Job Options

Job Options is another site that focuses on the IT professional. You can use Job Options to search by location, post your resumé, or read news about the technical industry. You can reach Job Options at www.joboptions.com. Figure 15-3 shows the home page for this site.

The Monster Board

The Monster Board is a huge resource for both technical and nontechnical jobs. You can search for jobs in a particular category or by geographic region. The Monster Board allows you to post your resumé on the site and also offers online job fairs. You can reach the Monster Board at www.monsterboard.com. For a look at the Monster Board home page, check out Figure 15-4.

Figure 15-3:
The Job
Options
home page.

Figure 15-4:
The
Monster
Board.

Career.Com

Career.Com offers a good resource for job searches and posting your resumé. This site doesn't focus solely on the IT professional industry, but you can find lots of information about companies here. Check it out at `www.career.com`. Figure 15-5 shows the home page for this site.

CareerExchange

Like Career.Com, this site doesn't focus only on IT professional jobs, but it does a good job of networking people together. You can find lots of information about recruiters here, as well as search for jobs and post your resumé. You can reach CareerExchange at `www.careerexchange.com`. Figure 15-6 shows the CareerExchange home page.

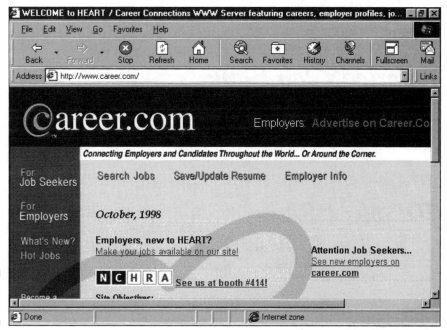

Figure 15-5:
Career.Com.

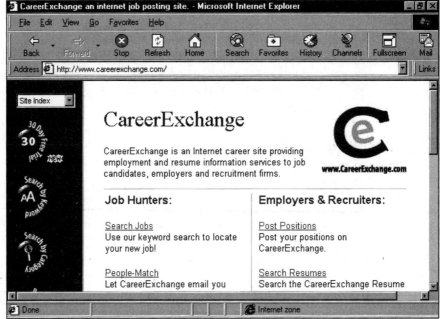

Figure 15-6:
Career-
Exchange.

America's Job Bank

America's Job Bank, shown in Figure 15-7, is a generalized site for a variety of professions. This site is a good starting point if you want to learn more about what's happening within various industries. You can search for jobs from this site and post your resumé online. Check it out at www.ajb.dni.us.

TOPjobs USA

TOPjobs USA is another generalized site that features a job search engine and an "Employee Mall." It's a good starting place, and you can reach the site at www.topjobsusa.com. Figure 15-8 shows the home page.

Job Safari

Job Safari is a giant index and search engine of companies and their staffing needs. This site is a good place to look for a particular company and openings the company may have. You can reach Job Safari at www.jobsafari.com, and Figure 15-9 shows the home page for this site.

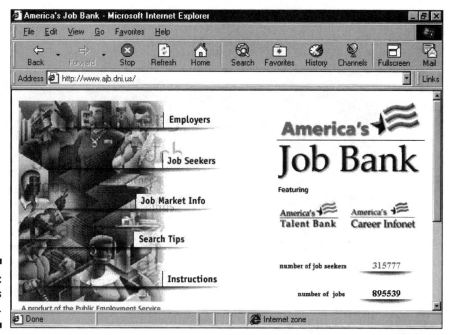

Figure 15-7:
America's
Job Bank.

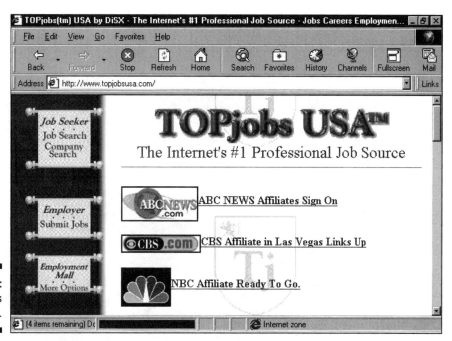

Figure 15-8:
TOPjobs
USA.

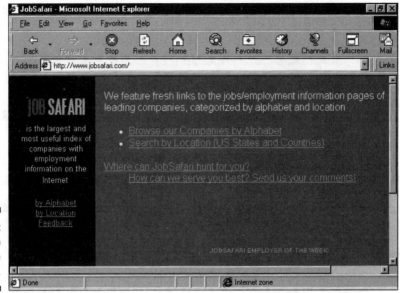

Figure 15-9:
The Job
Safari home
page.

Career Mosaic

Career Mosaic, shown in Figure 15-10, is another general job site. You can search for jobs by profession and location, and you can post your resumé on this site. Career Mosaic offers online job fairs and related services. Check it out at www.careermosaic.com.

Figure 15-10:
Career
Mosaic.

Chapter 16

Ten Questions You Must Ask during Your Job Interview

*Y*ou have an appointment with a prospective employer. Your research shows that this organization holds promise for the kind of work you want to do in the information technology field. You expect the employer to ask about your experience, skills, and certifications. You're also planning to pose your own set of questions, and this chapter offers ten good launching points for a conversation that can provide lots of insight into this company and the career opportunities it offers. You can ask these questions in any order, except the last one, which you need to save for last.

What Is a Typical Day Like for This Position?

First, you want to see if the interviewer's version matches the job description that you first noticed in the newspaper, online, or wherever. Secondly, a typical-day description gives you some basis for deciding whether you'd enjoy the job. Also, ask about the job priorities. The position may have several responsibilities, but what are the job's major priorities?

Will I Be "On Call"?

Many technology jobs — especially systems administrator jobs for small- to medium-sized companies — require *somebody* to troubleshoot the system when it breaks. Ask the company whether you have to wear a beeper. What happens if you're on a romantic getaway weekend and the system crashes? What happens if the system goes down while your family is out at the pizza parlor? Do you have to respond to every problem?

How Often Do You Do Salary Reviews and Performance Reviews?

It's okay to discuss salary and performance reviews, but you should let the interviewer bring up the topic of negotiating your salary. You undoubtedly expect performance and expertise to determine your salary, so you're likely to expect your first review after your first six months with the company. Hopefully, in the first six months, you can prove that your contributions are worth an increase. Thereafter, you can shoot for annual reviews.

Do You Offer Continuing Education and on What Terms?

Many companies gladly pay for your continuing education; however, your employer may ask you to sign a contract stating that you will pay the company back if you leave its employment within a certain period of time. This question may fall within your discussion of benefits, but the subject's important enough to your future to warrant a separate question.

What Are Your Plans for the MIS Department over the Next Five Years?

Want to know your advancement opportunities within the Management Information Systems area? Just ask this question to gauge the company's commitment to continuing growth and development.

How Long Have You Worked Here?

If your prospective boss is interviewing you, his or her length of service and range of experience within the organization give you clues about whether you can count on valid answers about the working environment.

How Would Employees Describe Working for This Company?

If everybody looks at each other or stumbles over their words answering this one, you may want to look elsewhere. Although a Pollyanna "everything's coming up roses" response is hardly realistic, a healthy, happy company generally prompts a fairly smooth and quick reply. Also, ask to visit with some employees after the interview. In this way, you can find out the "real story" about a company and get a feel for the people you will work with. If the interviewer seems uncomfortable with this idea, that's usually a bad sign.

How Many Employees Work in the MIS Department?

You can gauge workload distribution by this question. If the answer is 2, you can expect quite a bit of work, right?

What Benefits Does the Company Offer?

You're looking for such benefits as a 401k plan, profit-sharing, health and life insurance, stock options or a stock purchase plan, discounts, and paid vacations. No need to be embarrassed about bringing up benefits. This is your future we're talking about here. Also, benefits are an extra negotiating tool. If standard vacation is two weeks for the first year, negotiate an extra week instead of pushing for that $5,000 salary add-on.

Final Question — Ask this one only when the interview is over.

What Is the Best Time for Me to Call You?

Save this question until the interview's over. Always make an appointment to contact the employer with either your decision (to an offer) or additional questions. Your inquiry shows commitment and interest. Remember, a job interview is a sales call, because you're selling yourself. Treat it like that. Asking for a callback time is like making a follow-up call in sales. Seize the moment — this is your shot at a memorable first impression!

Part V
Appendixes

The 5th Wave   By Rich Tennant

"...and it doesn't appear that you'll have much trouble grasping some of the more 'alien' configuration concepts on this MCSE exam."

In this part . . .

*I*n the appendixes, you can find the inside scoop on taking your test preparation to the next logical step — actually scheduling your MCSE exam. To help you get ready for that big day, we also list the objectives for the core exams, and we provide a practice exam. The practice test is about the size of a regular MCSE exam and offers you a chance to apply the techniques that you explore in this book.

Appendix A
Scheduling Your MCSE Exam

In This Appendix

▶ Registering with either Sylvan Prometric or Virtual University Enterprises

▶ Checking out the exam premises

*W*hen you're ready to schedule your exam, you need to call either Sylvan Prometric or Virtual University Enterprises (VUE) to register and pay for the exam. The process is rather easy, and this appendix tells you exactly what to do!

Registering for Your MCSE Exam

Registering for an exam is extremely easy, either online or by telephone. Before you sign up, remember to visit the Microsoft Web site for any updates to the exams or testing policies. Here's the URL:

```
www.microsoft.com/Train_Cert/mcp/certstep/examreg.htm
```

When you register for an exam, you need to share the following specific information:

- ✔ Exam number
- ✔ Social Security number
- ✔ Your name
- ✔ Your address
- ✔ Your telephone number
- ✔ Your e-mail address
- ✔ Payment method (If paying by check, you must submit payment before you actually take the exam.)

Currently, all exams cost $100 each. Beta exams — that is, exams currently in development — cost $50. Two companies offer testing: Sylvan Prometric and Virtual University Enterprises.

You can schedule exams from one day to six weeks in advance. However, some testing centers may allow you to register up to 30 minutes before an exam. This last-minute signup is entirely at the center's discretion and depends upon space availability.

If you need to cancel an exam for any reason, you must cancel at least one working day in advance. Credits for missed exams are good for up to one year. As long as you meet the cancellation policy, you can receive a full refund. You cannot receive a refund for exams already taken.

Sylvan Prometric

Sylvan has more than 1,400 sites, domestic and international. You can register for exams online at the Internet address listed or through the toll-free number:

- ✔ **Internet Address:** www.prometric.com
- ✔ **Telephone:** USA, 800-755-EXAM (800-755-3926), or outside USA, 612-820-5707

Virtual University Enterprises (VUE)

You can register online or through the Internet address at www.vue.com/ms. Check the VUE Web site for locations:

- ✔ **Internet Address:** www.vue.com
- ✔ **Telephone Number:** 888-837-8616

Inspecting the Prospective Testing Center

We recommend that you choose one location for all your exams; registration is easier when it's focused on one test center because Sylvan or VUE will already have the testing information in your file. You also adapt to your testing environment after repeat visits and will feel more comfortable. You can find a testing center near you by speaking with the Sylvan Prometric or VUE representative on the phone or performing a search on either Web site.

However, you must find a testing center you like. You pick your favorite after you apply a little legwork, and, of course, answer every question on your checklist of things to look for!

- ✔ Schedule an appointment to visit the testing center. Explain that you're visiting to view the testing rooms and the facility in general. Of course, you need to schedule a time when no one is testing. Call late in the day one day before you want to visit. By that time, the testing center is likely to have a complete schedule for the next day's testing. If not, call early in the morning on the day that you plan to stop by.

- ✔ Ask to see the testing room. Request a few moments to sit in the room with the door closed. You want to gauge the amount of noise that you can hear with the door closed.

- ✔ Look for a testing center room without windows. Your test performance will benefit from lack of distractions outside — and you surely don't want people staring in at you.

- ✔ Stand outside the testing room for a few minutes. Do people linger outside the room and talk? Do you detect a lot of foot traffic from nearby ATEC classes? Did you hear any of this noise when you sat inside the room?

After you invest such a lot of work in this certification, the last thing you need is a noisy testing center.

Appendix B
Practice Exam

•••

Practice Exam Rules

▶ 90 minutes

▶ 50 questions

▶ Passing score: 35 or more correct answers

•••

*I*n this appendix, you enjoy an opportunity to take a unique practice exam. The test is unique because it's probably one of the few exercises that covers all the core exams and a couple of electives. You have a sampling of the entire spectrum of questions for many exams.

Question style and your general approach to the test format are vital considerations for exam success. Content is always important, too, because your answers depend on knowledge of the material. For this practice exam, focus carefully on each question's important elements and don't skimp on the quality of your work. Above all, pace yourself, moving as swiftly as you possibly can while taking enough time to analyze each question and answer option.

The answers for this practice exam appear at the end of the test. However, on the real thing, you don't have a chance to see the answers, only the results.

So have at it! Here's your MCSE practice exam.

Practice Exam

1 Which protocol is considered "connectionless?"

A ○ TCP/IP

B ○ UDP

C ○ IPX

D ○ NetBEUI

2 You install a new network adapter card in your computer, but the operating system cannot detect it. What is the most likely cause?

A ○ Mismatched DLLs

B ○ Incorrect protocol

C ○ Incorrect frame type

D ○ Incorrect IRQ setting

3 Which connectivity device can perform protocol conversion?

A ○ Routers

B ○ Brouters

C ○ Bridges

D ○ Gateways

4 You want to protect the data on your corporate server against a hard disk crash. The expense or loss of storage space is not an issue; the data must be protected.

Required Result: Implement a software-based fault-tolerant solution.

Optional Desired Result: The solution should be easy to implement with NT Server 4.

Proposed Solution: Implement Raid Level 5.

A ○ The solution produces both the desired result and the optional result.

B ○ The solution produces only the desired result.

C ○ The solution produces only the optional result.

D ○ The solution does not produce either the desired result or the optional result.

5 Which layer of the OSI model contains both the LLC and MAC sublayers?

A ○ Application

B ○ Transport

C ○ Data Link

D ○ Physical

6 Which network access method broadcasts a message telling the other computers that it intends to send data over the wire?

A ○ Token Ring
B ○ CSMA/CD
C ○ CSMA/CA
D ○ CSMA/CX

7 What can be used during a Windows NT automated installation to automatically answer some of the user prompts?

A ○ Request File
B ○ Answer File
C ○ Response File
D ○ Data File

8 You want 10 Macintosh computers on your network to be able to access the NT Server. What two items must be installed on the NT Server to allow this to happen? (Choose two.)

A ❑ AppleTalk Protocol
B ❑ AppleNet Protocol
C ❑ Services for Macintosh
D ❑ File and print services for Apple

9 If the PDC becomes unavailable, which computer would become the Browse Master for the network?

A ○ BDC
B ○ Member Server
C ○ NT Workstation
D ○ Windows 95

10 Your C: drive contains Windows NT and is formatted with NTFS. You now want to return the drive to FAT.

Required Result: Remove NTFS and return to FAT.

Optional Desired Result: Avoid reinstalling the operating system and applications.

Proposed Solution: Run FDISK.EXE to reconfigure the C: drive to FAT, then reformat the drive.

A ○ The proposed solution produces the required result and the optional result.
B ○ The proposed solution produces only the required result.
C ○ The proposed solution produces only the optional result.
D ○ The proposed solution does not produces the required result or the optional result.

11 You have been having some problems with a particular application on your Windows NT computer. You would like NT to create a crash dump file whenever an application error occurs so you can troubleshoot the problem. How do you do this?

A ○ Choose the recovery option in MSINFO32

B ○ Choose the recovery option in Dr. Watson

C ○ Choose the recovery option in NetWatcher

D ○ Select the crash dump file option in Performance Monitor

12 To configure a mandatory roaming user profile, how should NTUSER.DAT be renamed?

A ○ NTUSERMAN.DAT.

B ○ NTUSERROAM.MAN.

C ○ NTUSER.MAN.

D ○ No change is required.

13 You manage a print server at your office. You have just received an updated driver for the printer and you need to install it.

Required Result: Update the printer driver for the print server and the client computers.

Optional Desired Result: Perform this task in the easiest, most efficient manner.

Proposed Solution: Update the driver on the print server and do nothing more.

A ○ The proposed solution produces both the required result and the optional result.

B ○ The proposed solution produces only the required result.

C ○ The proposed solution produces only the optional result.

D ○ The proposed solution does not produce either the required result or the optional result.

14 You are an administrator for a mixed NT/NetWare environment. One of the client computers has client services for NetWare installed, but the password needs to be changed on the NetWare 3.*x* server. How can you perform this action?

A ○ By changing the password in User Manager for Domains

B ○ By changing the password in the Network applet in Control Panel

C ○ By using the Setpass utility on the NetWare Server

D ○ By using the PASSREQ.EXE utility on the NetWare Server

15 In a company that has 60 computers on the network divided into three departments, what is the best domain model if centralized account administration is necessary?

A ○ Single Domain
B ○ Multiple Domain
C ○ Multiple Master Domain
D ○ Workgroup

16 You want to allow your NT clients to print on a printer on a NetWare server. What must be installed on the NT server that authenticates the clients to allow this to happen? (Choose all that apply.)

A ❑ SAP
B ❑ File and Print Services for NetWare
C ❑ Server Services for NetWare
D ❑ NWLink Protocol

17 You work in a building where power outages are frequent. What should you use to protect your server against the power outages?

A ○ USP
B ○ UPS
C ○ Volume Set
D ○ Implement Crash Data Save Options

18 What is a small, fast, efficient protocol developed by Microsoft?

A ○ TCP/IP
B ○ NetBIOS
C ○ NetBEUI
D ○ DLC

19 You are an administrator for a large NT network. You want to configure the network so that when clients log on, they are automatically assigned an IP address. What service should you use to accomplish this?

A ○ WINS
B ○ DNS
C ○ SMTP
D ○ DHCP

20 In your network, you have 200 Windows NT computers and 5 UNIX servers. The NT computers are WINS enabled, and you would like to resolve computer names with minimal use of static name resolution. What is the best way to accomplish this?

A ○ Set up DNS to use WINS
B ○ Set up DNS to use TCP
C ○ LMHOSTS file
D ○ HOSTS file

21 What is required to implement disk duplexing?

A ○ One physical disk and two controllers
B ○ Two physical disks
C ○ Two physical disks and two disk controllers
D ○ One physical disk and one controller

22 What is another name for a Windows NT fault-tolerance feature sometimes called "hot fixing"?

A ○ RAID 0
B ○ RAID 5
C ○ Sector Sparing
D ○ Disk Mirroring

23 You have set up a dual-boot configuration with Windows NT Server and Windows 95. While in Windows 95, you are unable to see drive D:, where you installed NT Server. What is the most likely reason?

A ○ You cannot dual boot NT and 95.
B ○ You formatted the file system as FAT32.
C ○ You formatted the file system as NTFS.
D ○ You are using different protocols.

24 What network troubleshooting tool uses sonar-like pulses to look for a break or short in the cable?

A ○ DVM
B ○ TDR
C ○ Line Tracer
D ○ Protocol Analyzer

25 What network troubleshooting tool can capture and read packets?

A ○ Advanced Cable Tester
B ○ DVM
C ○ Oscilloscope
D ○ Protocol Analyzer

26 You want to resolve NetBIOS names to IP addresses on your local NT network. What service is needed for this?

A ○ DNS
B ○ DHCP
C ○ WINS
D ○ Ipconfig

27 You set up a dual-boot computer with Windows 95 and Windows NT Workstation. However, you never receive the boot menu screen and the computer automatically boots to Windows 95. How can you resolve this problem?

A ○ By defragmenting the FAT partition.

B ○ By manually editing NTDETECT.COM to change the timeout value.

C ○ By manually editing NTLDR to change the timeout value.

D ○ By manually editing the BOOT.INI file to change the timeout value.

28 You want to protect sensitive files on your computer. You allow other office workers to use your workstation periodically throughout the day. You want to secure these files so that they cannot be read by unauthorized users. Your computer dual boots Windows 95 and Windows NT Workstation. Both operating systems use FAT16.

Required Result: Secure files from unauthorized users.

Optional Desired Result: Avoid major system changes.

Proposed Solution: Implement NTFS security and secure the directory with the sensitive files so it cannot be accessed by unauthorized users.

A ○ The solution produces both the required result and the optional result.

B ○ The solution produces the required result only.

C ○ The solution produces the optional result only.

D ○ The solution does not produce either the required result or the optional result.

29 What is the best way to upgrade Windows 95 to Windows NT while preserving all settings?

A ○ Run winnt.exe and install NT in the same directory.

B ○ Run winnt32.exe and install NT in the same directory.

C ○ Convert the partition to NTFS and run winnt32.exe.

D ○ There is no upgrade path from Windows 95 to Windows NT.

30 You want to be able to print to an Apple LaserWriter connected to a Macintosh computer from your Windows NT workstation. What protocol is needed to accomplish this?

A ○ AppleTalk

B ○ ApplePrint

C ○ AppleServe

D ○ TCP/IP

31 Your printer is shared with a number of coworkers. You want to allow them to use the printer, but you want your print jobs to have priority. How can you accomplish this?

A ○ Create a separate printer for yourself with the priority set to 1.

B ○ Create a separate printer for yourself with the priority set to 99.

C ○ Choose deferred printing for your print jobs.

D ○ This cannot be done.

32 In which Registry key would you find information about your modem?

A ○ HKEY_LOCAL_MACHINE

B ○ HKEY_DYN_DATA

C ○ HKEY_USERS

D ○ HKEY_CURRENT_CONFIG

33 You suspect that there is a duplicate NetBIOS name error on your network after receiving an `Event 4320, NetBT Error` message. What command can you use at your NT Server computer to confirm or deny this?

A ○ ping 127.0.0.1

B ○ netstat -a

C ○ nbtstat -n

D ○ arp-a

34 What DNS file provides the IP addresses of the nine domain name servers that provide root-level name resolution in the United States?

A ○ root.dom.

B ○ cache.dns.

C ○ LMHOSTS.

D ○ This information is not resolved in DNS.

35 When configuring RAS to connect to an ISP, what IP setting on the RAS server is not needed?

A ○ IP address

B ○ Subnet Mask

C ○ Default Gateway

D ○ Cache

36 What protocol should you enable in a TCP/IP network to configure routing tables with the least amount of administrative effort?

A ○ WINS

B ○ RIP

C ○ DHCP

D ○ ARP

37 Which of the following are considered fault-tolerant solutions? (Choose all that apply.)

A ❑ Volume Sets
B ❑ RAID 1
C ❑ RAID 5
D ❑ Disk Duplexing

38 Your network contains UNIX systems and Windows NT. What is the best protocol to use in this network?

A ○ TCP/IP
B ○ IPX
C ○ NetBEUI
D ○ AppleTalk

39 Your Windows NT Server contains a SCSI disk and an IDE disk. Each disk contains one primary partition. The boot partition is on the SCSI disk. Which of the following is the correct ARC name for the boot partition?

A ○ scsi (0) disk (0) rdisk (0) partition (1)
B ○ scsi (0) disk (1) rdisk (0) partition (1)
C ○ scsi (0) disk (0) rdisk (1) partition (2)
D ○ scsi (1) disk (1) rdisk (0) partition (1)

40 In networks that use NWLink, what is a common connectivity problem?

A ○ Mismatched protocols
B ○ Incorrect frame type
C ○ Incorrect packet addressing
D ○ Incorrect MAC addressing

41 What product provides both content caching for Internet resources and a secure firewall against unauthorized users?

A ○ DHCP server
B ○ WINS server
C ○ IIS server
D ○ Proxy Server

42 If you have Windows NT auditing for logon activities enabled, what can you use to see which users have made unsuccessful logon attempts?

A ○ Performance Monitor
B ○ NetWatcher
C ○ Event Viewer
D ○ Network Monitor

43 Your network contains Windows 95 computers. You would like to implement user-level security. What will your network need to accomplish this?

A ○ A WINS server

B ○ A Windows NT server

C ○ Appropriate share permissions

D ○ A proxy server

44 You need to use SLIP with a dial up networking connection. Which protocols can be transmitted with SLIP using Windows 95?

A ○ TCP/IP

B ○ IPX

C ○ PPTP

D ○ DLC

45 Which protocol is an application-layer protocol?

A ○ FTP

B ○ IP

C ○ NWLink

D ○ NetBEUI

46 Which type of cable uses modulated light pulses to send data?

A ○ 10Base2

B ○ 10BaseX

C ○ 10BaseT

D ○ Fiber Optic

47 Your network uses twisted pair cabling. What kind of connector is used for twisted pair?

A ○ AUI

B ○ RJ-11

C ○ RJ-45

D ○ BNC

48 What are standard, formatted packets that contain instructions required by Windows NT Server service?

A ○ MNC

B ○ SMB

C ○ NetBIOS

D ○ DTG

49 Which layer of the OSI model takes raw data bits and organizes them into frames?

A ○ Application

B ○ Transport

C ○ Data Link

D ○ Physical

50 The 10Base5 topology is often referred to as _____.

A ○ Fast Ethernet

B ○ Standard Ethernet

C ○ Token Ring

D ○ Workgroup

Answers

1 *B. UDP.* User Datagram Protocol is considered a connectionless protocol. It makes a "best effort" in transmitting data, but the connection and delivery are not guaranteed.

2 *D. Incorrect IRQ setting.* The most likely cause of a NIC detection failure is an incorrect IRQ setting on the NIC. If this setting is unavailable on the computer, the operating system cannot detect the NIC.

3 *D. Gateways.* A gateway is the only device that can perform protocol conversion between two LANs.

4 *A. The solution produces both the desired result and the optional result.* Raid Level 5 provides fault-tolerant disk striping with parity. This solution is software based and easy to implement using NT Server 4.

5 *C. Data Link.* The Data Link layer contains the LLC and MAC sublayers.

6 *C. CSMA/CA.* CSMA/CA (Carrier Sense Multiple Access with Collision Avoidance) broadcasts a message to the other computers telling them that it intends to send data. This access method is not as popular as CSMA/CD and Token Ring because of the broadcast traffic. CSMA/CX is a bogus answer.

7 *B. Answer file.* Answer files can be used in automated installations of Windows NT to automatically install some or even all of the user prompts during a normal installation.

8 *A and C. AppleTalk Protocol* and *Services for Macintosh.* In order to enable Macintosh computers to connect to an NT server, the NT server must have the AppleTalk protocol and Services for Macintosh installed.

9 *A. BDC.* In the event that the PDC becomes unavailable, a browser election may be called. If this occurs, the BDC will win the Browse Master election because of its role in the network.

10 *B. The proposed solution produces only the required result.* The only way to return a drive to FAT from NTFS is to run FDISK and reformat the drive. This does, of course, erase the operating system, applications, and all data.

11 *B. Choose the recovery option in Dr. Watson.* Dr. Watson for Windows NT can be used to diagnose application errors and log those errors to a crash dump file.

12 *C. NTUSER.MAN.* To configure a mandatory roaming user profile, the file must be copied to a shared directory and renamed to NTUSER.MAN. This prevents the user from making changes to the profile and saving them.

13 *A. The proposed solution produces both the required result and the optional result.* The easiest way to update a printer driver on a network printer is to simply update the driver on the print server. The client computers will automatically receive the updated driver when they try to print to the print server.

14 *C. By using the Setpass utility on the NetWare Server.* Because this is a NetWare 3.*x* server, it is bindery-based to maintain security. The Setpass utility can be used on NetWare servers using bindery emulation to make changes to passwords.

15 *A. Single Domain.* A single domain model is best for this arrangement. Considering the size of the network and the need for centralized administration, the single domain model will work best.

16 *B and D. File and Print Services for NetWare* and *NWLink protocol.* For communication, NWLink is required. Because the clients also need printer services, File and Print Services for NetWare must also be installed.

17 *B. UPS.* If power outages are a problem, an UPS (Uninterruptible Power Supply) should be used. The UPS can provide the server with enough power to perform an orderly shutdown.

18 *C. NetBEUI.* NetBEUI is the Microsoft proprietary protocol. It is fast and efficient and particularly useful on smaller LANs, but it's not a routable protocol.

19 *D. DHCP.* DHCP (Dynamic Host Configuration Protocol) enables you to automatically assign IP addresses to network clients, thus eliminating the need for static IP address configuration.

20 *A. Set up DNS to use WINS.* You can configure DNS to use WINS, which will dynamically resolve computer names. In this way, you can use the advantages of WINS in the absence of an NT Server.

21 *C. Two physical disks and two disk controllers.* Disk duplexing is an enhancement to disk mirroring. The minimum requirement is two physical disks, each with its own disk controller. This design protects against both disk and controller failure.

22 *C. Sector Sparing.* Sector Sparing, or hot fixing, is an advanced NT Server feature that attempts to move data out of bad sectors in the file system and relocate it on the fly.

23 *C. You formatted the file system as NTFS.* Windows 95 cannot read NTFS partitions. If Windows 95 is unable to see the D drive, then in all likelihood, the drive is formatted as NTFS.

24 *B. TDR.* A TDR (Time Domain Reflectometer) uses sonarlike pulses to find a break, short, or imperfection in the cable that may hinder performance.

25 *D. Protocol Analyzer.* The Protocol Analyzer is the only tool that can capture, decode, and read packets.

26 *C. WINS.* WINS (Windows Internet Naming Service) is a dynamic service that can resolve NetBIOS computer names to IP addresses. WINS leases an IP address to a computer for use on the network. This service eliminates the need to manually track the NetBIOS name to IP address for each machine.

27 *D. By manually editing the BOOT.INI file to change the timeout value.* If the boot menu fails to appear in a dual-boot configuration, the BOOT.INI timeout value is probably set to 0. This setting tells BOOT.INI how long to wait before choosing the default operating system. Most timeout values are set to 30, giving the user 30 seconds to select the operating system desired.

28 *D. The solution does not produce either the required result or the optional result.* Because the dual-boot configuration uses the FAT file system, you cannot implement NTFS. Although you can convert the NT Workstation partition to NTFS, NTFS is not supported in Windows 95.

29 *D. There is no upgrade path from Windows 95 to Windows NT.* Because no upgrade path exists, the only option is to run winnt.exe and install NT in a different directory. Then, you have to manually reinstall all applications and manually move all files.

30 *A. AppleTalk.* Macintosh printers use the AppleTalk protocol.

31 *B. Create a separate printer for yourself with the priority set to 99.* You can create different printers for the same print device with different priority levels set. A print priority of 99 gives your documents priority over all other documents.

32 *A. HKEY_LOCAL_MACHINE.* You can find all hardware and system setting information in HKEY_LOCAL_MACHINE.

33 *C. Nbtstat -n.* Nbtstat -n displays the name of a computer that has a duplicate IP address on the network.

34 *B. Cache.dns.* Cache.dns provides the root-level resolution for the domain names, such as com, net, edu, and mil.

35 *C. Default Gateway.* When configuring RAS to connect to an ISP, a default gateway setting is not configured because this information is provided by the ISP.

36 *B. RIP.* RIP (Routing Information Protocol) can be used in TCP/IP networks to automatically configure and maintain network routing tables.

37 *B, C, and D. RAID 1, RAID 5, and Disk Duplexing.* RAID 1, RAID 5, and Disk Duplexing are all considered fault-tolerant solutions in that data can be recovered in the case of hardware failure. Volume sets are storage solutions; however, they do not provide any fault tolerance.

38 *A. TCP/IP.* For interoperability with UNIX systems, TCP/IP is the standard, routable protocol that should be used.

39 A. *scsi(0)disk(0)rdisk(0)partition(1).* The ARC name for a SCSI drive follows the following format: scsi (x) disk (y) rdisk (z) partition (a). The number after scsi is the original number of the hardware adapter card, beginning with zero. The number after rdisk is always zero for a scsi controller. The number after partition is the original number of the partition, beginning with one.

40 B. *Incorrect frame type.* Most protocols automatically determine the packet type to be used. NWLink is the exception. The IPX protocol is not tied to any particular frame type, and incorrect frame types are common network problems in this environment.

41 D. *Proxy Server.* Microsoft Proxy Server (2) provides content caching to speed network access to the Internet and a secure firewall.

42 C. *Event Viewer.* If NT auditing for logon activities is enabled, you can view unsuccessful logon attempts in Event Viewer.

43 B. *A Windows NT Server.* In order to implement user-level security, you must have a security provider, such as an NT server. Users are authenticated by the server to gain access to shares on the Windows 95 machines.

44 A. *TCP/IP.* SLIP (Serial Line Internet Protocol) is an older connection protocol that only supports TCP/IP in Windows 95.

45 A. *FTP.* FTP (File Transfer Protocol) is an application layer protocol (those that work at the upper layer of the OSI model). The other choices work at lower levels of the OSI model.

46 D. *Fiber Optic.* Fiber optic cable uses modulated pulses of light which are sent through a glass cladding to communicate. Fiber Optic has the highest transmission distance (2,000 meters) and is highly secure, although rather expensive.

47 C. *RJ-45.* RJ-45 connectors are used for twisted pair.

48 B. *SMB.* SMB (Server Message Blocks) are high-level formats for packets that are used by Windows NT Server.

49 C. *Data Link.* Data bits are organized into data frames at the Data Link Layer of the OSI model. Header and trailer information (such as the CRC) are also added at this layer.

50 B. *Standard Ethernet.* The 10Base5 topology is generally referred to as standard Ethernet or thicknet. 10Base5 is typically used as a backbone to connect network segments.

Appendix C
Web Sites to Remember

. . . .

In This Appendix

▶ Important Web sites to bookmark

. . . .

*I*n this appendix, we recap what we feel are the most important Web sites that we mention throughout the book. Bookmark these Web sites so that you check them periodically as you work on your MCSE. For each site, we include the URL, a brief description, and a look at the site's opening page.

MCP

First and foremost, train yourself to visit the MCP Web site regularly; you can find it at `www.microsoft.com/mcp`. This site can keep you abreast of what's happening in the Microsoft certification world. You get up-to-the-minute news, information on new or retired certifications, and most importantly, the Exam Preparation Guides. See Figure C-1 for a preview of the MCP home page.

Certification Steps

Do you need some additional guidance as you work on your MCSE? Then the Microsoft Certification Steps site is for you. The Certification Steps site provides you with detailed information on planning and conquering your certification track. You can reach this site at `www.microsoft.com/mcp/certsteps/steps.htm`. Figure C-2 shows you the home page.

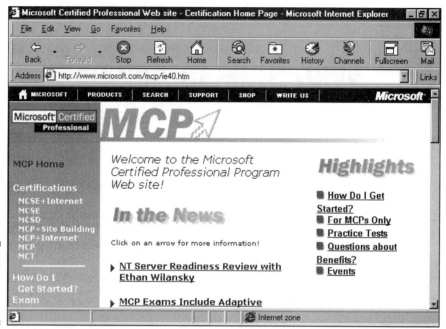

Figure C-1:
Check the
MCP home
page often.

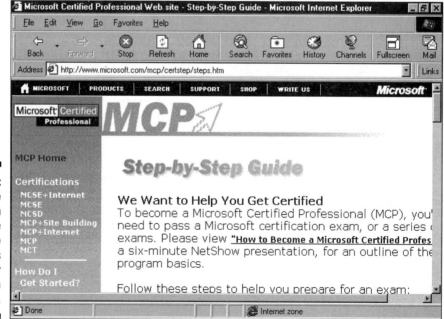

Figure C-2:
The
Certification
Steps home
page
supports
your
certification
trek.

Training and Certification

If you want information about training options as well as the Microsoft strategic certification and training plans, visit the Training and Certification site. This site can provide you with additional training information and give you a look at some of Microsoft's new initiatives. You can access the site at `www.microsoft.com/train_cert`; check out the home page in Figure C-3.

MCT

The MCT, Microsoft Certified Trainer, is a companion certification to other Microsoft technical certifications. The MCT certifies instructors to teach Microsoft Official Curriculum courses. If you're interested in the MCT certification and want to keep current about the training industry, then check out `www.microsoft.com/mct`. Figure C-4 shows you the home page.

Figure C-3:
A world of information awaits at the Training and Certification site.

Figure C-4:
The MCT
site gives
you the
inside
news on
becoming a
certified
trainer.

TechNet

The TechNet Web site offers you a look at the Microsoft TechNet program, which you receive free on CD-ROM for one year when you earn your MCSE certification. As you work on your MCSE, however, you can find out more about Microsoft technologies online through the TechNet Web site. Visit the site at www.microsoft.com/technet and preview the home page in Figure C-5.

MCP Magazine

Are you wondering what your MCSE is really worth? Do you want to keep up with industry changes for MCSEs? Then visit www.mcpmag.com. This site provides a detailed look into the world of Microsoft certifications. The home page appears in Figure C-6.

Figure C-5:
Don't miss
the TechNet
Web site!

Figure C-6:
Study MCP
Magazine
for
certification
insight.

Windows NT Magazine

You can access the *Windows NT Magazine* Web site at www.winntmag.com. This Web site, although not directly focused on certification, can keep you up-to-date on developments in the Windows NT world. You can find out about using NT in various environments and discover what's coming your way in future releases of Windows NT. Figure C-7 shows the *Windows NT Magazine* home page.

Saluki

The best nonofficial Web site dedicated to the MCP is www.saluki.com/mcp. This site offers a wealth of information about Microsoft certifications, technical discussions, and even various e-mail subscription lists. See Figure C-8 for the Saluki home page.

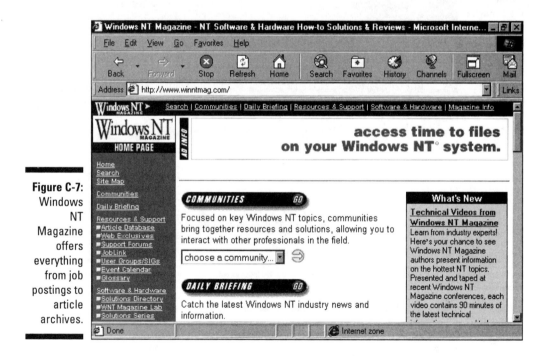

Figure C-7:
Windows
NT
Magazine
offers
everything
from job
postings to
article
archives.

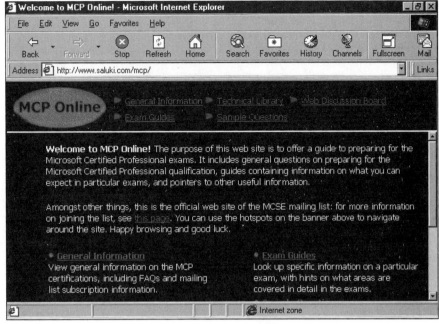

Figure C-8:
Visit the
Saluki site
as you
prepare for
your
exams.

Appendix D

Exam Objectives for the Core MCSE Exams

● ●

In This Appendix

▶ Exam Objectives for Exam 70-067, Implementing and Supporting Microsoft Windows NT Server 4.0

▶ Exam Objectives for Exam 70-068, Implementing and Supporting Microsoft Windows NT Server 4.0 in the Enterprise

▶ Exam Objectives for Exam 70-058, Networking Essentials

▶ Exam Objectives for Exam 70-064, Implementing and Supporting Microsoft Windows 95

▶ Exam Objectives for Exam 70-098, Implementing and Supporting Microsoft Windows 98

▶ Exam Objectives for Exam 70-073, Implementing and Supporting Microsoft Windows NT Workstation 4.0

● ●

As you prepare for each MCSE certification exam, pattern your studies after the objectives that Microsoft lists in the corresponding exam preparation guide. Each exam preparation guide names the skills that you must master to pass a particular exam.

In this appendix, we provide the exam objectives for the core MCSE exams. You should also take a look at Chapter 3, which details the requirements for MCSE certification. We compiled this information from the exam preparation guides that were available when we wrote this book. Exam requirements can change, so you may want to check the Microsoft Web site for the latest versions of the exam preparation guides.

To find the exam preparation guides online, follow these steps:

1. **Go to the Microsoft Training and Certification Web site, at the following address:**

   ```
   www.microsoft.com/train_cert/
   ```

2. **Click the Find an Exam link.**

3. **On the search page that's displayed, use the drop-down lists to select the product and the certification that you want.**

4. **Click the link for the exam that you want.**

   You see the exam preparation guide for the selected exam.

If you need information on any exam, you can call the MCP Hotline at 800-636-7544.

Note: The exam lengths and passing scores that we list in this appendix are estimates. Those details vary from exam to exam, and Microsoft changes exam content and passing score expectations periodically.

Each exam question counts evenly. Questions are not weighted — in other words, one question does not count more than any others.

Exam Preparation Guide for Exam 70-067, Implementing and Supporting Microsoft Windows NT Server 4.0

This certification exam measures your ability to implement, administer, and troubleshoot information systems that incorporate Windows NT Server Version 4.0 in a simple computing environment. A simple computing environment is typically a homogeneous LAN, which may include one or more servers, a single domain, and a single location. The LAN may have file-sharing and print-sharing capabilities.

Here are the details about this exam:

- **Internet address:** www.microsoft.com/mcp/exam/stat/sp70-067.htm
- **Exam length:** 90 minutes
- **Total number of questions:** approximately 55 to 65
- **Passing score:** 764 out of 1,000, answering approximately 43 to 50 questions correctly

Before taking this exam, you need to develop proficiency in the following job skills.

Planning

✔ Plan the disk drive configuration for various requirements. Requirements include

- Choosing a file system

- Choosing a fault-tolerance method

✔ Choose a protocol for various situations. Protocols include

- TCP/IP

- NWLink IPX/SPX Compatible Transport

- NetBEUI

Installation and configuration

✔ Install Windows NT Server on Intel-based platforms.

✔ Install Windows NT Server to perform various server roles. Server roles include

- Primary domain controller

- Backup domain controller

- Member server

✔ Install Windows NT Server by using various methods. Installation methods include

- CD-ROM

- Over-the-network

- Network Client Administrator

- Express versus custom

✔ Configure protocols and protocol bindings. Protocols include

- TCP/IP

- NWLink IPX/SPX Compatible Transport

- NetBEUI

✔ Configure network adapters. Considerations include

- Changing IRQ, IObase, and memory addresses

- Configuring multiple adapters

✔ Configure Windows NT Server core services. Services include

- Directory Replicator
- License Manager
- Other services

✔ Configure peripherals and devices. Peripherals and devices include

- Communication devices
- SCSI devices
- Tape device drivers
- UPS devices and UPS service
- Mouse drivers, display drivers, and keyboard drivers

✔ Configure hard disks to meet various requirements. Requirements include

- Allocating disk space capacity
- Providing redundancy
- Improving performance
- Providing security
- Formatting

✔ Configure printers. Tasks include

- Adding and configuring a printer
- Implementing a printer pool
- Setting print priorities

✔ Configure a Windows NT Server computer for various types of client computers. Client computer types include

- Windows NT Workstation
- Microsoft Windows 95
- Microsoft MS-DOS-based

Managing resources

✔ Manage user and group accounts. Considerations include

- Managing Windows NT groups
- Managing Windows NT user rights

- Managing Windows NT groups
- Administering account policies
- Auditing changes to the user account database

✔ Create and manage policies and profiles for various situations. Policies and profiles include

- Local user profiles
- Roaming user profiles
- System policies

✔ Administer remote servers from various types of client computers. Client computer types include

- Windows 95
- Windows NT Workstation

✔ Manage disk resources. Tasks include

- Copying and moving files between file systems
- Creating and sharing resources
- Implementing permissions and security
- Establishing file auditing

Connectivity

✔ Configure Windows NT Server for interoperability with NetWare servers by using various tools. Tools include

- Gateway Service for NetWare
- Migration Tool for NetWare

✔ Install and configure Remote Access Service (RAS). Configuration options include

- Configuring RAS communications
- Configuring RAS protocols
- Configuring RAS security
- Configuring Dial-Up Networking clients

Monitoring and optimization

✔ Monitor performance of various functions by using Performance Monitor. Functions include

- Processor
- Memory
- Disk
- Network

✔ Identify performance bottlenecks

Troubleshooting

✔ Choose the appropriate course of action for resolving installation failures.

✔ Choose the appropriate course of action for resolving boot failures.

✔ Choose the appropriate course of action for resolving configuration errors.

✔ Choose the appropriate course of action for resolving printer problems.

✔ Choose the appropriate course of action for resolving RAS problems.

✔ Choose the appropriate course of action for resolving connectivity problems.

✔ Choose the appropriate course of action for resolving resource access problems and permission problems.

✔ Choose the appropriate course of action for resolving fault-tolerance failures. Fault-tolerance methods include

- Tape backup
- Mirroring
- Stripe set with parity
- Disk duplexing

Exam Preparation Guide for Exam 70-068, Implementing and Supporting Microsoft Windows NT Server 4.0 in the Enterprise

This certification exam measures your ability to implement, administer, and troubleshoot information systems that incorporate Windows NT Server Version 4.0 in an enterprise computing environment. An enterprise computing environment is typically a heterogeneous WAN, which may include multiple servers and multiple domains. The enterprise environment may run sophisticated server applications.

Here's a rundown on the details of this exam:

- ✔ **Internet address:** www.microsoft.com/mcp/exam/stat/sp70-068.htm
- ✔ **Exam length:** 90 minutes
- ✔ **Total number of questions:** approximately 50 to 65
- ✔ **Passing score:** 784 out of 1,000, answering approximately 40 to 51 questions correctly

The exam focuses on the following job skills.

Planning

- ✔ Plan the implementation of a directory services architecture. Considerations include
  - • Selecting the appropriate domain model
  - • Supporting a single logon account
  - • Allowing users to access resources in different domains
- ✔ Plan the disk drive configuration for various requirements. Requirements include choosing a fault-tolerance method.
- ✔ Choose a protocol for various situations. Protocols include
  - • TCP/IP
  - • TCP/IP with DHCP and WINS

- NWLink IPX/SPX Compatible Transport Protocol
- Data Link Control (DLC)
- AppleTalk

Installation and configuration

✔ Install Windows NT Server to perform various server roles. Server roles include

- Primary domain controller
- Backup domain controller
- Member server

✔ Configure protocols and protocol bindings. Protocols include

- TCP/IP
- TCP/IP with DHCP and WINS
- NWLink IPX/SPX Compatible Transport Protocol
- DLC
- AppleTalk

✔ Configure Windows NT Server core services. Services include

- Directory Replicator
- Computer Browser

✔ Configure hard disks to meet various requirements. Requirements include

- Providing redundancy
- Improving performance

✔ Configure printers. Tasks include

- Adding and configuring a printer
- Implementing a printer pool
- Setting print priorities

✔ Configure a Windows NT Server computer for various types of client computers. Client computer types include

- Windows NT Workstation
- Windows 95
- Macintosh

Managing resources

✔ Manage user and group accounts. Considerations include

- Managing Windows NT user accounts
- Managing Windows NT user rights
- Managing Windows NT groups
- Administering account policies
- Auditing changes to the user account database

✔ Create and manage policies and profiles for various situations. Policies and profiles include

- Local user profiles
- Roaming user profiles
- System policies

✔ Administer remote servers from various types of client computers. Client computer types include

- Windows 95
- Windows NT Workstation

✔ Manage disk resources. Tasks include

- Creating and sharing resources
- Implementing permissions and security
- Establishing file auditing

Connectivity

✔ Configure Windows NT Server for interoperability with NetWare servers by using various tools. Tools include

- Gateway Service for NetWare
- Migration Tool for NetWare

✔ Install and configure multiprotocol routing to serve various functions. Functions include

- Internet router
- BOOTP/DHCP Relay Agent
- IPX router

✔ Install and configure Internet Information Server.

✔ Install and configure Internet services. Services include

- World Wide Web

- DNS

- Intranet

✔ Install and configure Remote Access Service (RAS). Configuration options include

- Configuring RAS communications

- Configuring RAS protocols

- Configuring RAS security

Monitoring and optimization

✔ Establish a baseline for measuring system performance. Tasks include creating a database of measurement data.

✔ Monitor performance of various functions by using Performance Monitor. Functions include

- Processor

- Memory

- Disk

- Network

✔ Monitor network traffic by using Network Monitor. Tasks include

- Collecting data

- Presenting data

- Filtering data

✔ Identify performance bottlenecks.

✔ Optimize performance for various results. Results include

- Controlling network traffic

- Controlling server load

Troubleshooting

✔ Choose the appropriate course of action for resolving installation failures.

✔ Choose the appropriate course of action for resolving boot failures.

✔ Choose the appropriate course of action for resolving configuration errors. Tasks include

- Backing up and restoring the Registry
- Editing the Registry

✔ Choose the appropriate course of action for resolving printer problems.

✔ Choose the appropriate course of action for resolving RAS problems.

✔ Choose the appropriate course of action for resolving connectivity problems.

✔ Choose the appropriate course of action for resolving resource access and permission problems.

✔ Choose the appropriate course of action for resolving fault-tolerance failures. Fault-tolerance methods include

- Tape backup
- Mirroring
- Stripe set with parity

✔ Perform advanced problem resolution. Tasks include

- Diagnosing and interpreting a blue screen
- Configuring a memory dump
- Using the Event Log service

Exam Preparation Guide for Exam 70-058, Networking Essentials

This certification exam measures your ability to implement, administer, and troubleshoot information systems that incorporate Microsoft Windows 95 and any products in the Microsoft BackOffice family. The exam covers only the networking knowledge and skills common to both Windows 95 and BackOffice products.

Here are the details about this exam:

✔ **Internet address:** www.microsoft.com/mcp/exam/stat/ sp70-058.htm

✔ **Exam length:** 60 to 75 minutes

✔ **Total number of questions:** approximately 60 to 75

✔ **Passing score:** 793 out of 1,000, answering approximately 48 to 61 questions correctly

The exam expects you to demonstrate proficiency in the following job skills.

Standards and terminology

✔ Define common networking terms for LANs and WANs.

✔ Compare a file-and-print server with an application server.

✔ Compare user-level security with access permission assigned to a shared directory on a server.

✔ Compare a client/server network with a peer-to-peer network.

✔ Compare the implications of using connection-oriented communications with connectionless communications.

✔ Distinguish whether SLIP or PPP is used as the communications protocol for various situations.

✔ Define the communication devices that communicate at each level of the OSI model.

✔ Describe the characteristics and purpose of the media used in IEEE 802.3 and IEEE 802.5 standards.

✔ Explain the purpose of NDIS and Novell ODI network standards.

Planning

✔ Select the appropriate media for various situations. Media choices include

- Twisted-pair cable
- Coaxial cable
- Fiber-optic cable
- Wireless

Situational elements include

- Cost
- Distance limitations
- Number of nodes

✔ Select the appropriate topology for various token-ring and Ethernet networks.

✔ Select the appropriate network and transport protocol or protocols for various token-ring and Ethernet networks. Protocol choices include

- DLC
- AppleTalk
- IPX
- TCP/IP
- NFS
- SMB

✔ Select the appropriate connectivity devices for various token-ring and Ethernet networks. Connectivity devices include

- Repeaters
- Bridges
- Routers
- Brouters
- Gateways

✔ List the characteristics, requirements, and appropriate situations for WAN connection services. WAN connection services include

- X.25
- ISDN
- Frame relay
- ATM

Implementation

✔ Choose an administrative plan to meet specified needs, including performance management, account management, and security.

✔ Choose a disaster recovery plan for various situations.

✔ Given the manufacturer's documentation for the network adapter, install, configure, and resolve hardware conflicts for multiple network adapters in a token-ring or Ethernet network.

✔ Implement a NetBIOS naming scheme for all computers on a given network.

✔ Select the appropriate hardware and software tools to monitor trends in the network.

Troubleshooting

✔ Identify common errors associated with components required for communications.

✔ Diagnose and resolve common connectivity problems with cards, cables, and related hardware.

✔ Resolve broadcast storms.

✔ Identify and resolve network performance problems.

Exam Preparation Guide for Exam 70-064, Implementing and Supporting Microsoft Windows 95

This certification exam measures your ability to implement, administer, and troubleshoot information systems that incorporate Windows 95, and it measures your ability to provide technical support to users of Windows 95. This exam is based on the version of Windows 95 that Microsoft released August 24, 1995 (build 950).

Here are the details about this exam:

✔ **Internet address:** `www.microsoft.com/mcp/exam/stat/sp70-064.htm`

✔ **Exam length:** 90 minutes

✔ **Total number of questions:** approximately 55 to 65

✔ **Passing score:** 764 out of 1,000, answering approximately 41 to 50 questions correctly

Before taking the exam, you need to become proficient in the following job skills.

Planning

✔ Develop an appropriate implementation model for specific requirements. Considerations include choosing a workgroup configuration or logging on to an existing domain.

✔ Develop a security strategy. Strategies include

- System policies
- User profiles
- File and printer sharing

Installation and configuration

✔ Install Windows 95. Installation options include

- Automated Windows setup
- New
- Upgrade
- Uninstall
- Dual-boot combination with Microsoft Windows NT

✔ Install and configure the network components of a client computer and server.

✔ Install and configure network protocols. Protocols include

- NetBEUI
- IPX/SPX-compatible protocol
- TCP/IP
- Microsoft DLC
- PPTP/VPN

✔ Install and configure hardware devices. Hardware devices include

- Modems
- Printers

✔ Configure system services, including browser services.

✔ Install and configure backup hardware and software. Hardware and software include

- Tape drives
- The Backup application

Configuring and managing resource access

✔ Assign access permissions for shared folders. Methods include

- Passwords
- User permissions
- Group permissions

✔ Create, share, and monitor resources. Resources include

- Remote
- Network printers
- Shared fax modem
- Unimodem/V

✔ Set up user environments by using user profiles and system policies.

✔ Back up data and restore data.

✔ Manage hard disks. Tasks include

- Disk compression
- Partitioning

✔ Establish application environments for Microsoft MS-DOS applications.

Integration and interoperability

✔ Configure a Windows 95 computer as a client computer in a Windows NT network.

✔ Configure a Windows 95 computer as a client computer in a NetWare network.

✔ Configure a Windows 95 computer to access the Internet.

✔ Configure a client computer to use Dial-Up Networking for remote access.

Monitoring and optimization

✔ Monitor system performance. Tools include

- NetWatcher
- System Monitor

✔ Tune and optimize the system. Tools include

- Disk Defragmenter
- ScanDisk
- DriveSpace

Troubleshooting

✔ Diagnose and resolve installation failures.

✔ Diagnose and resolve boot process failures.

✔ Diagnose and resolve connectivity problems. Tools include

- WinIPCfg
- Net Watcher
- Troubleshooting wizards

✔ Diagnose and resolve printing problems.

✔ Diagnose and resolve file system problems.

✔ Diagnose and resolve resource access problems.

✔ Diagnose and resolve hardware device and device driver problems. Tools include

- MSD
- Add/Remove Hardware Wizard

✔ Perform direct modification of the Registry as appropriate by using REGEDIT.

Exam Preparation Guide for Exam 70-098, Implementing and Supporting Microsoft Windows 98

This certification exam measures your ability to implement, administer, and troubleshoot information systems that incorporate Microsoft Windows 98, and it measures your ability to provide technical support to users of Windows 98.

Here are the details about this exam:

✔ **Internet address:** www.microsoft.com/mcp/exam/stat/ sp70-098.htm

✔ **Exam length:** 90 minutes

✔ **Total number of questions:** approximately 55 to 65

✔ **Passing score:** 764 out of 1,000, answering approximately 44 to 50 questions correctly

The exam is a test of your proficiency in the following job skills.

Planning

✔ Develop an appropriate implementation model for specific requirements in a Microsoft environment or a mixed Microsoft and NetWare environment. Considerations include

- Choosing the appropriate file system
- Planning a workgroup

✔ Develop a security strategy in a Microsoft environment or a mixed Microsoft and NetWare environment. Strategies include

- System policies
- User profiles
- File and printer sharing
- Share-level access control or user-level access control

Installation and configuration

✔ Install Windows 98. Installation options include

- Automated Windows setup
- New
- Upgrade
- Uninstall
- Dual-boot combination with Microsoft Windows NT 4.0

✔ Configure Windows 98 server components. Server components include

- Microsoft Personal Web Server 4.0
- Dial-Up Networking server

✔ Install and configure the network components of Windows 98 in a Microsoft environment or a mixed Microsoft and NetWare environment. Network components include

- Client for Microsoft Networks
- Client for NetWare Networks
- Network adapters
- File and printer sharing for Microsoft Networks
- File and printer sharing for NetWare Networks
- Service for NetWare Directory Services (NDS)
- Asynchronous Transfer Mode (ATM) components
- Virtual private networking and PPTP
- Browse Master

✔ Install and configure network protocols in a Microsoft environment or a mixed Microsoft and NetWare environment. Protocols include

- NetBEUI
- IPX/SPX-compatible protocol
- TCP/IP
- Microsoft DLC
- Fast Infrared

✔ Install and configure hardware devices in a Microsoft environment and a mixed Microsoft and NetWare environment. Hardware devices include

- Modems
- Printers
- Universal Serial Bus (USB)
- Multiple display support
- IEEE 1394 Firewire
- Infrared Data Association (IrDA)
- Multilink
- Power management scheme

✔ Install and configure Microsoft Backup.

Managing resources

✔ Assign access permissions for shared folders in a Microsoft environment or a mixed Microsoft and NetWare environment. Methods include

- Passwords
- User permissions
- Group permissions

✔ Create, share, and monitor resources. Resources include

- Remote computers
- Network printers

✔ Set up user environments by using user profiles and system policies.

✔ Back up data and the Registry and restore data and the Registry.

✔ Configure hard disks. Tasks include

- Disk compression
- Partitioning
- Enabling large disk support
- Converting to FAT32

✔ Create hardware profiles

Connectivity

✔ Configure a Windows 98 computer as a client computer in a network that contains a Windows NT 4.0 domain.

✔ Configure a Windows 98 computer as a client computer in a NetWare network.

✔ Configure a Windows 98 computer for remote access by using various methods in a Microsoft environment or a mixed Microsoft and NetWare environment. Methods include

- Dial-Up Networking
- Proxy Server

Monitoring and optimization

✔ Monitor system performance by using NetWatcher, System Monitor, and Resource Meter.

✔ Tune and optimize the system in a Microsoft environment and a mixed Microsoft and NetWare environment. Tasks include

- Optimizing the hard disk by using Disk Defragmenter and ScanDisk

- Compressing data by using DriveSpace 3 and the Compression Agent

- Updating drivers and applying service packs by using Windows Update and the Signature Verification Tool

- Automating tasks by using Maintenance Wizard

- Scheduling tasks by using Task Scheduler

- Checking for corrupt files and extracting files from the installation media by using the System File Checker

Troubleshooting

✔ Diagnose and resolve installation failures. Tasks include resolving file and driver version conflicts by using Version Conflict Manager and the Microsoft System Information utility.

✔ Diagnose and resolve boot process failures. Tasks include editing configuration files by using System Configuration Utility.

✔ Diagnose and resolve connectivity problems in a Microsoft environment and a mixed Microsoft and NetWare environment. Tools include

- Winipcfg
- NetWatcher
- Ping
- Tracert

✔ Diagnose and resolve printing problems in a Microsoft environment or a mixed Microsoft and NetWare environment.

✔ Diagnose and resolve file system problems.

✔ Diagnose and resolve resource access problems in a Microsoft environment or a mixed Microsoft and NetWare environment.

✔ Diagnose and resolve hardware device and device driver problems. Tasks include checking for corrupt Registry files by using ScanReg and ScanRegW.

Exam Preparation Guide for Exam 70-073, Implementing and Supporting Microsoft Windows NT Workstation 4.0

This certification exam measures your ability to implement, administer, and troubleshoot information systems that incorporate Windows NT Workstation Version 4.0.

Here are the details about this exam:

- **Internet address:** www.microsoft.com/mcp/exam/stat/sp70-073.htm
- **Exam length:** 90 minutes
- **Total number of questions:** approximately 55 to 70
- **Passing score:** 705 out of 1,000, answering approximately 39 to 50 questions correctly

Before taking the exam, you should be proficient in the following job skills.

Planning

- Create unattended installation files.
- Plan strategies for sharing and securing resources.
- Choose the appropriate file system to use in a given situation. File systems and situations include
  - NTFS
  - FAT
  - HPFS
  - Security
  - Dual-boot systems

Installation and configuration

- Install Windows NT Workstation on an Intel platform in a given situation.
- Set up a dual-boot system in a given situation.
- Remove Windows NT Workstation in a given situation.

✔ Install, configure, and remove hardware components for a given situation. Hardware components include

- Network adapter drivers
- SCSI device drivers
- Tape device drivers
- UPS
- Multimedia devices
- Display drivers
- Keyboard drivers
- Mouse drivers

✔ Use Control Panel applications to configure a Windows NT Workstation computer in a given situation.

✔ Upgrade to Windows NT Workstation 4.0 in a given situation.

✔ Configure server-based installation for wide-scale deployment in a given situation.

Managing resources

✔ Create and manage local user accounts and local group accounts to meet given requirements.

✔ Set up and modify user profiles.

✔ Set up shared folders and permissions.

✔ Set permissions on NTFS partitions, folders, and files.

✔ Install and configure printers in a given environment.

Connectivity

✔ Add and configure the network components of Windows NT Workstation.

✔ Use various methods to access network resources.

✔ Implement Windows NT Workstation as a client in a NetWare environment.

✔ Use various configurations to install Windows NT Workstation as a TCP/IP client.

✔ Configure and install Dial-Up Networking in a given situation.

✔ Configure Microsoft Peer Web Services in a given situation.

Running applications

✔ Start applications on Intel and RISC platforms in various operating system environments.

✔ Start applications at various priorities.

Monitoring and optimization

✔ Monitor system performance by using various tools.

✔ Identify and resolve a given performance problem.

✔ Optimize system performance in various areas.

Troubleshooting

✔ Choose the appropriate course of action to take when the boot process fails.

✔ Choose the appropriate course of action to take when a print job fails.

✔ Choose the appropriate course of action to take when the installation process fails.

✔ Choose the appropriate course of action to take when an application fails.

✔ Choose the appropriate course of action to take when a user cannot access a resource.

✔ Modify the Registry using the appropriate tool in a given situation.

✔ Implement advanced techniques to resolve various problems.

Bonus Practice Exam

. . . .

Practice Exam Rules

▶ 90 minutes

▶ 50 questions

▶ Passing score: 35 or more correct answers

. . . .

*H*ere you have it! A full bonus exam to practice your skills and get an inside glimpse at the kinds of questions you'll encounter on the real Microsoft certification exams. Like the sample exam in Appendix B, this bonus practice exam covers topics from all the core exams and a couple of electives. You have a sampling of the entire spectrum of questions for many exams.

Question style and your general approach to the test format are vital considerations for exam success. Content is always important, too, because your answers depend on knowledge of the material. For this practice exam, focus carefully on each question's important elements and don't skimp on the quality of your work. Above all, pace yourself, moving as swiftly as you possibly can while taking enough time to analyze each question and answer option.

The answers for this practice exam appear at the end of the test. However, on the real thing, you don't have a chance to see the answers, only the results.

Bonus Practice Exam

1 Which of the following is a valid UNC name that can be used to map a share on a remote server to the local computer? (Choose two.)

A ❑ \\ntsrv101\ipc$

B ❑ \\ntsvr101\c*

C ❑ \\ntsrv101

D ❑ \\ntsrv101\files

2 Your company network consists of 100 Microsoft Windows NT Workstation computers, three NT Servers, and 50 UNIX clients. Which of the following protocols will enable you to communicate among all of them?

A ○ DLC

B ○ NWLink

C ○ TCP/IP

D ○ NetBEUI

3 Which of the following are valid switches for the Windows NT unattended setup?

A ○ /ox

B ○ /rd

C ○ /udf

D ○ /udl

4 Which utility do you use to find out whether you have correctly installed TCP/IP?

A ○ ping 127.0.0.1

B ○ ping 127.0.0.0

C ○ ping 126.0.0.1

D ○ telnet 127.0.0.1

5 Which OSI layer contains the IP protocol?

A ○ Transport

B ○ Application

C ○ Session

D ○ Network

6 You are running a network containing a mirror set with a logical drive letter of D. You come to work one morning, and note that the primary drive of the mirror set has failed. What steps must you take to correct this problem?

A ○ Install another hard disk, then boot the computer with a floppy disk that has a boot.ini file pointing to the hard disk that has not failed. In Server Manager, choose Break Mirror. Then, after you configure the new drive, choose Regenerate to rebuild the mirror.

B ○ Install another hard disk and then boot the computer with a floppy disk that has a boot.ini file pointing to the hard disk that has not failed. In Disk Administrator, choose Break Mirror. Then, after you configure the new drive, choose Regenerate to rebuild the mirror.

C ○ Install another hard disk and then boot the computer with a floppy disk that has a boot.ini file pointing to the hard disk that has not failed. In Server Manager for Domains, choose Break Mirror. Then, after you configure the new drive, choose Recreate Mirror Set to rebuild the mirror.

D ○ Install another hard disk and then boot the computer with a floppy disk that has a boot.ini file pointing to the hard disk that has not failed. In Disk Administrator, choose Break Mirror. Then, after you configure the new drive, choose Recreate Mirror Set to rebuild the mirror.

7 The domain containing the data that users in another domain want to access is called the _____:

A ○ Trusted domain

B ○ Master domain

C ○ Resource domain

D ○ Trusting domain

8 If you are interested in capturing packet information between two computers, you should use _____:

A ○ Performance Monitor

B ○ Protocol Analyzer

C ○ Network Monitor

D ○ Tracert

9 Your environment consists of five Windows 95 machines, 12 Windows NT Workstations, and 10 NetWare clients, all using a single NT Server that is set up as a print server. The printer manufacturer releases a new driver for the printer. How should you apply this driver?

A ○ At all workstations and the print server

B ○ At just the workstations

C ○ At just the server

D ○ Do not install the driver, because it will disable all NetWare clients

10 What type of fiber-based network uses tokens like a token ring to communicate?

A ○ SONET

B ○ X.25

C ○ 100 VG AnyLAN

D ○ FDDI

11 Which of the following devices is used simply to boost and clarify the signal being sent across the network?

A ○ Repeater

B ○ Router

C ○ Bridge

D ○ Hub

12 You have a file in Partition A, and you want to move it to Partition B. Will the file inherit the permissions of the folder on the target partition, or will it retain its own permissions?

A ○ It will retain its own permissions.

B ○ The administrator will be given the option of assigning it the permissions of the target folder, but the default is for the folder to retain its own permissions.

C ○ It will inherit the permissions of the target folder.

D ○ A file cannot be moved between partitions.

13 You are the administrator for a small network that has Windows NT Workstations, Windows NT Servers, and UNIX Workstations. In this environment, you use TCP/IP as your only protocol. Until now, the NT machines have been able to communicate with each other, and the UNIX machines have been able to talk to each other. You are asked by management to recommend the best way to perform name resolution so that all of these computers can communicate on the network. What is your recommendation?

A ○ Create an LMHosts file on each computer, statically mapping the name of each workstation to its IP address.

B ○ Install WINS, and have each computer log onto the network. Because WINS is updated dynamically, the database will be built automatically, enabling all computers to communicate.

C ○ Install DNS, and have each computer log onto the network. Because DNS is updated dynamically, the database will be built automatically, enabling all computers to communicate.

D ○ Install WINS, and create static IP address mappings for UNIX computers. All Windows NT computers will be updated automatically when they log onto the network.

14 What does ARP do?

A ○ Provides for NetBIOS name to IP address mapping

B ○ Provides for host name to IP address mapping

C ○ Provides for MAC address to IP address mapping

D ○ Provides for NetBIOS name to host name mapping

15 You are the administrator of a network consisting of three separate segments. Each segment is separated by a router. Segments A and B each have 20 Windows NT Workstations and one Windows NT Server acting as a Backup Domain Controller. On segment C, you have 50 Windows NT Workstations and one Windows NT Server acting as the Primary Domain Controller as well as the DHCP server. Your entire network should obtain its IP addresses from the DHCP server. What must you do so that computers on segments A and B can receive their IP addresses from the DHCP server on segment C?

A ○ Do nothing. When a computer logs on, it will broadcast its request for an IP address, and DHCP will reply with one automatically.

B ○ In order for segments A and B to receive addresses from DHCP, the Boot P protocol must be installed on each of the routers.

C ○ In order for segments A and B to receive addresses from DHCP, the Boot P protocol must be installed on each of the routers. Additionally, one computer on each of segments A and B must be configured as a DHCP Relay Agent.

D ○ In order for segments A and B to receive addresses from DHCP, a DHCP server must be installed on each segment.

16 _____ multitasking occurs when the operating system determines the amount of time one application is allowed to access the CPU before access is cut off and given to another application.

A ○ Cooperative

B ○ Preeminent

C ○ Preferential

D ○ Pre-emptive

17 Which view of Performance Monitor enables you to create a record of computer activity that can be saved and reviewed later?

A ○ Report

B ○ Log

C ○ Alert

D ○ Chart

18 You are the administrator of a small Windows NT domain. Currently, you have 300 Windows NT Workstations and two Windows NT Servers. One of the servers functions as the Primary Domain Controller, and the other acts as a file and print server. Your company buys out a competitor, and hires its staff, thus doubling the size of the company. Management asks you to add the new staff members' computers to the network. To do so, you determine that you need a Backup Domain Controller to handle all logon requests. What must you do with the Windows NT Server that currently acts a file and print server if you want to upgrade it to a BDC for the domain?

A ○ Open Server Manager on the file and print server, and choose Upgrade to Backup Domain Controller.

B ○ Open Server Manager on the file and print server, and choose Synchronize Directories with the Primary Domain Controller.

C ○ Open Server Manager on the Primary Domain Controller, and modify the Hardware Profile of the file and print server to be a Backup Domain Controller.

D ○ Reinstall the file and print server as a Backup Domain Controller, then reinstall all applications and settings.

19 The two modes of operation within a Windows NT computer are _____.

A ○ User and kernel

B ○ User and protected

C ○ Kernel and protected

D ○ User and Win32 subsystem

20 Your environment includes 30 NetWare clients and one NetWare 3.11 server. You want to have your NetWare environment begin communicating with a Windows NT domain in the adjacent building. The Windows NT domain consists of one Windows NT Server and 50 Windows NT Workstations. The Windows NT Workstations should communicate only with the Windows NT Server. How should you set up your environment to enable the two networks to communicate?

A ○ Install Client Services for NetWare on each of the Windows NT Workstations, and have them connect directly to the NetWare server.

B ○ Install Gateway Services for NetWare on the Windows NT Server, and Client Services for NetWare on each of the Windows NT Workstations. Have each of the workstations connect to the Windows NT Server computer, and have the Windows NT Server computer talk to the NetWare server.

C ○ Install Gateway Services for NetWare on the Windows NT Server. Have each of the workstations connect to the Windows NT Server computer, and have the Windows NT Server computer talk to the NetWare server.

D ○ Install File and Print Services for NetWare on the Windows NT Server. Have each of the workstations connect to the Windows NT Server computer, and have the Windows NT Server computer talk to the NetWare server.

21 You have been asked to install a new Windows NT Server to your existing network. This Windows NT Server will hold Microsoft SQL Server 6.5, and will be accessed by numerous administrators and developers. How should you configure the properties of your Server service?

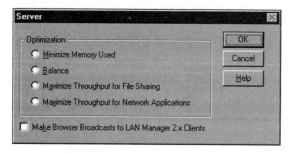

A ○ Minimize Memory Used

B ○ Balance

C ○ Maximize Throughput for File Sharing

D ○ Maximize Throughput for Network Applications

22 You need to configure your computer with a new hardware profile, so that it will not try to connect to the network upon startup when you are traveling. What are the steps necessary to create a new hardware profile?

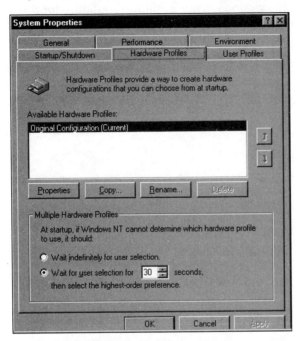

A ○ Click Properties, and reconfigure the existing hardware profile to disable the Network Card when you're traveling.

B ○ Click Copy, and rename the existing hardware profile. Open the properties of the new hardware profile and select the appropriate options. Reboot the computer.

C ○ Click Rename, and give the hardware profile a name that describes it as the profile to use when traveling. Then click Properties, and configure the profile to disable the Network Card when you're traveling.

D ○ Nothing needs to be done. The existing hardware profile will cause Windows NT to send out a broadcast upon startup to see if it is connected to the network. If it is not, then the Network Card will be disabled automatically.

23 You are configuring your computer as a Windows NT Server that will function as the Primary Domain Controller of a medium-sized network. Your Windows NT Server will have only 32MB of memory. What are the minimum and maximum pagefile settings that you should configure for this machine? Enter your answer in the appropriate places in the dialog box that's displayed here:

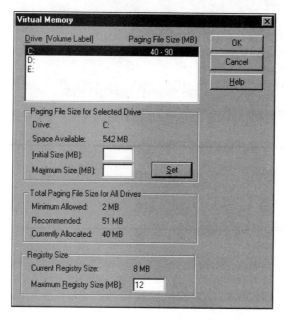

24 You have just added two new hard drives to your Windows NT Server. You are very adept at keeping up-to-date disaster recovery records for your computer. What should you do to update the Emergency Repair Disk that you keep for this computer?

A ○ Run RDISK.EXE from the command prompt.

B ○ Run DrWTSN32 –I from the command prompt.

C ○ Rerun setup, select 'R' for repair, and insert the Emergency Repair Disk to update it with the new information.

D ○ Insert the Emergency Repair Disk and reboot the machine. Upon reboot, the new information will be automatically copied to the disk.

25 You install a new video driver in you Windows NT Workstation. When you reboot the computer and log on, you find that the screen is totally unreadable. How can you troubleshoot this situation?

A ○ Log off and log back on with the Last Known Good option.

B ○ Log off and log back on a second time. The computer should note the problem, and try to correct it automatically.

C ○ From the command prompt, remove the offending driver and reinstall the old one.

D ○ Log off and log back on using the VGA mode option, then remove the offending driver.

26 You print to a NetWare printer on a NetWare Server on your NT Network. You run Windows NT Workstation. You would like to be informed when your print jobs have printed. What do you need to do to receive this notification?

A ○ Check the Notify When Printed option in the Printer Properties window.

B ○ In the Client Service for NetWare, check the Notify When Printed option.

C ○ The NetWare Server must be configured to provide this notification.

D ○ This action cannot be done using a NetWare Server.

27 Which command line utility can you use to view NetBIOS over IP statistics and information on your network?

A ○ ping

B ○ Netstat

C ○ Nbtstat

D ○ Ipconfig

28 Your network contains 800 client machines and several NT Servers. Your users need to access the Internet for their work. You want to allow one of the NT Servers to process all Internet requests.

Required Result: All users should gain access through one link through one of the NT Servers.

Optional Desired Result: The Server should provide security against Internet intrusion.

Proposed Solution: Install Proxy Server 2.0 on a dedicated server and configure the clients to use the Proxy Server for Internet access. Enable IP Forwarding and configure a cache drive for performance.

A ○ The solution produces both the required result and the optional result.

B ○ The solution produces the required result only.

C ○ The solution produces the optional result only.

D ○ The solution does not produce either the required result or the optional result.

29 In Disk Administrator, shown in the following figure, which menu should you use to establish a mirror set?

```
Disk Administrator                                                    _ 8 X
Partition  Fault Tolerance  Tools  View  Options  Help

 ═══ Disk 0    C:
                FAT                                    Free Space
     1227 MB    1225 MB                                2 MB

 ═══ Disk 1    D:
                NTFS              Free Space
     697 MB     696 MB            1 MB

 ═══ Disk 2    E:
                FAT
     407 MB     406 MB

 ═══ CD-ROM 0  F:
                NTSRV40A
                CDFS
     611 MB     611 MB

 ■ Primary partition    ■ Logical drive
 Logical drive                        406 MB     FAT              E:
```

A ○ Partition

B ○ Fault Tolerance

C ○ Tools

D ○ Options

30 Which protocol can be used to enable NT computers to communicate with an IBM mainframe?

A ○ AppleTalk

B ○ IPX

C ○ DLC

D ○ TCP/IP

31 How can you view information about STOP events in Windows NT Workstation?

A ○ Performance Monitor

B ○ Network Monitor

C ○ Event Viewer

D ○ This information cannot be viewed.

32 What character can be added to a share name to make the share a hidden share?

A ○ %
B ○ #
C ○ @
D ○ $

33 What is the default subnet mask for a Class A network?

A ○ 255.0.0.0
B ○ 255.255.0.0
C ○ 255.255.255.0
D ○ 255.255.255.255

34 How do you use Performance Monitor to view physical disk object counters from a remote machine if you are an administrator and your Server is a domain member?

A ○ DiskPerf -Y
B ○ DiskPerf -A
C ○ DiskPerf -N
D ○ DiskPerf -C

35 Which cabling can be used to communicate within a distance of up to 500 meters without a repeater?

A ○ 10Base2
B ○ 10Base5
C ○ Fiber Optic
D ○ SONET

36 You need full access to a share on an NT network. You ask the administrator to grant you full access, and the administrator gives you this right. However, you still do not have full access to the share. What should you do?

A ○ Ask the administrator to unlock your account.
B ○ Ask the administrator to rename your account.
C ○ Change your password.
D ○ Log off and log back on.

37 You make changes to your display settings, and the screen goes blank during the test. Which of the following could cause this problem? (Choose all that apply.)

A ❑ The video card is not installed correctly.
B ❑ The Desktop Area setting is incorrect.
C ❑ A GP fault has occurred.
D ❑ The Color Palette setting is incorrect.

38 A router does not pass _____ messages to other network segments.

A ○ Broadcast

B ○ IP

C ○ NWLink

D ○ AppleTalk

39 You want certain entries in your LMHOSTS file to load into the name cache. What statement should you use with these entries so they are loaded into the name cache?

A ○ #DOM

B ○ #PRE

C ○ #CACHE

D ○ No action is necessary. All LMHOSTS names are loaded into cache memory.

40 Your company now has three divisions with approximately 1,000 users in each division. You want to centralize the administration of all user accounts, but you want to decentralize the management of local resources. Which domain model should you implement for your company?

A ○ Single Master Domain

B ○ Three-way Trust

C ○ Multiple Master Domain

D ○ This configuration cannot be done.

41 In the following Properties sheet, what should be changed to obtain an IP address from an NT Server?

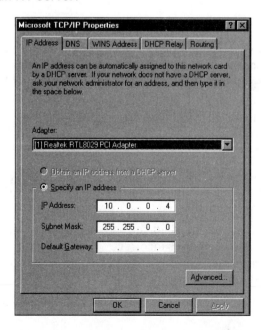

A ○ Enter the default gateway of the NT Server.
B ○ Enter the IP address of the NT Server.
C ○ Click the Obtain an IP address from a DHCP server button.
D ○ This cannot be done.

42 You are using four drives as a stripe set with parity, for a total drive size of 800MB. What percentage of the total drive size will be used for the parity bit?

A ○ $\frac{1}{2}$
B ○ $\frac{1}{4}$
C ○ $\frac{1}{3}$
D ○ $\frac{2}{3}$

43 What kind of network is created when using PPTP to send LAN packets over the Internet?

A ○ Local area network
B ○ Wide area network
C ○ Local hidden network
D ○ Virtual private network

44 What system should be used to resolve domain names, such as www.microsoft.com?

A ○ TCP/IP
B ○ WINS
C ○ DHCP
D ○ DNS

45 You copy a folder on an NTFS partition on your Windows NT Workstation to another NTFS partition on another NT Workstation. What will be the permissions of the copied folder?

A ○ The same permissions as the original.
B ○ The permissions of the target folder.
C ○ No Access.
D ○ The permissions must be reconfigured.

46 What is the minimum number of disks required to implement disk striping with parity?

A ○ 2
B ○ 3
C ○ 4
D ○ 5

47 Which tool works at the Physical layer of the OSI model and can be used to gather beaconing information?

A ○ Advanced Cable Tester

B ○ TDR

C ○ Protocol Analyzer

D ○ Beaconing information cannot be gathered

48 In the RAS Server TCP/IP Configuration, shown in the following figure, which option should you select to restrict dial-in clients to the Server only?

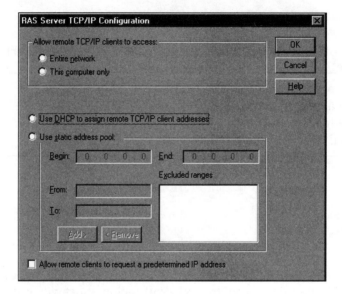

A ○ Entire Network

B ○ This Computer Only

C ○ Use Static Address Pool

D ○ Allow Remote Clients to Request a Predetermined IP Address

49 If a Windows NT Workstation computer will not boot properly, what should be done?

A ○ Boot in Safe Mode

B ○ Run the emergency repair process by booting from the setup disks

C ○ Use the Last Known Good Configuration

D ○ Format the drive

50 You want to allow the dynamic resolution of NetBIOS names to IP addresses on your TCP/IP network. What should you use to accomplish this?

A ○ WINS   C ○ DHCP

B ○ DNS   D ○ NetBIOSTRANS

Answers

1 *A and D. \\ntsrv101\ipc$ and \\ntsrv101\files.* When entering a UNC name, the standard is *\\servername\sharename.* The share in answer A is valid because it is a hidden, administrative share created on all NT computers. The $ means that the share is hidden and administrative. Answer B is incorrect due to the *, which is a forbidden character in NT naming schemes.

2 *C. TCP/IP.* DLC enables communication with mainframes. NWLink is for NetWare machines, and NetBEUI is a non-routable protocol for use by NT and IBM networks.

3 *C. /udf.* The /ox option enables you to create your three-disk installation set, but it has nothing to do with unattended installations. /rd and /udl are not recognized switches. /udf points to a file that contains information specific to each computer, and is used to specify the correct information to install on each computer.

4 *A. ping 127.0.0.1* When you ping 127.0.0.1, you are pinging the TCP/IP loopback address, which tells whether you have installed TCP/IP correctly. You can verify the installation of Telnet by connecting to a specified IP Address, but 127.0.0.1 is not a valid computer, and thus the telnet session would fail.

5 *D. Network.* The IP protocol, part of the TCP/IP suite, is a network level protocol.

6 *B. Install another hard disk and then boot the computer with a floppy disk that has a boot.ini file pointing to the hard disk that has not failed. In Disk Administrator, choose Break Mirror. Then, after you configure the new drive, choose Regenerate to rebuild the mirror.* To correct the problem, you must go into Disk Administrator. When rebuilding the mirror set, you must choose Regenerate.

7 *D. Trusting domain.* In order for users to access the data, the domain containing the data must be set up as trusting the user domain. The data may or may not exist in a dedicated resource domain. The master domain holds user accounts.

8 *C. Network Monitor.* Network Monitor enables you to capture and view packets sent from one computer to another across the network.

9 *C. At just the server.* You just need to install the updated driver at the server.

10 *D. FDDI.* The FDDI network is a ring-based network that uses fiber cable to communicate.

11 *A. Repeater.* The repeater does little else than boost the signal that is being affected by attenuation. The other devices listed may also boost the signal, but that isn't their sole function.

12 *C. It will inherit the permissions of the target folder.* When you move a file between partitions, a physical change occurs on the hard disk. It first copies the file to another physical location, then it returns and deletes the file from the initial location. Any time a physical change is made to the file on the hard disk, the file will inherit the permissions of the target folder. This change takes place because a new object is being created, with no preexisting permissions.

13 *D. Install WINS and create static IP address mappings for UNIX computers. All Windows NT computers will be updated automatically when they log onto the network.* UNIX machines do not automatically register themselves with WINS, but can be manually entered into the WINS database. DNS is an appropriate name resolution method for both UNIX and NT machines, but is not dynamically updated. An LMHosts file will enable you to statically map any computers using NetBIOS names. UNIX machines do not use NetBIOS, but instead use Host names.

14 *C. Provides for MAC address to IP address mapping.* ARP (Address Resolution Protocol) is used, after the IP address is obtained, to request the hardware address (also called the MAC address) of the destination computer. It does not provide for name to IP address resolution.

15 *C. In order for segments A and B to receive addresses from DHCP, the Boot P protocol must be installed on each of the routers. Additionally, one computer on each of segments A and B must be configured as a DHCP Relay Agent.* Computers that are using DHCP supplied information will broadcast their requests for IP address information when they log on. If a router is separating the client from the DHCP server, however, the broadcast will not be passed to the DHCP server. In order for clients to successfully receive DHCP information, a computer on the local segment must be configured to listen to DHCP request broadcasts from new clients. The DHCP Relay Agent intercepts the broadcasts, and forwards them to the DHCP server across the router. To pass this information to the DHCP server, the router must have the Boot P protocol installed on it.

16 *D. Preemptive.* Preemptive multitasking occurs when the operating system determines how much time each application is allowed to access the CPU. Windows NT uses this type of multitasking. In cooperative multitasking, the application determines whether it wants to release its hold on the CPU, thus allowing other applications access.

17 *B. Log.* The log view enables you to record computer performance and store it for later reference. The log that's created can be viewed in Chart, and Reports can be created from it.

18 *D. Reinstall the file and print server as a Backup Domain Controller, then reinstall all applications and settings.* To upgrade a Windows NT Server from a non-domain controller to a domain controller, you must reinstall the operating system.

19 A. *User and kernel.* The two modes of operation are user and kernel mode. Applications can only operate in the user mode, with appropriate subsystems sending application and user requests to the kernel mode, so that it can receive operating system attention.

20 C. *Install Gateway Services for NetWare on the Windows NT Server. Have each of the workstations connect to the Windows NT Server computer, and have the Windows NT Server computer talk to the NetWare server.* Gateway Services for NetWare enables the Windows NT Server computer to communicate with the NetWare environment. Because all Windows NT Workstation clients should communicate with the Windows NT Server computer, no additional software is required for these computers.

21 D. *Maximize Throughput for Network Applications.* When a computer will be used for a network enabled application, such as SQL Server or Microsoft Exchange server, the Server service should be configured to Maximize Throughput for Network Applications.

22 B. *Click Copy, and rename the existing hardware profile. Open the properties of the new hardware profile, and select the appropriate options. Reboot the computer.* To create a hardware profile to disable your network card when traveling, you must copy the default one, and reconfigure the properties of the copy. The properties of the default hardware profile typically should not be altered, because these settings represent the way the computer will be initialized by default each time it starts.

23 The answer here is to remember that a pagefile should be set to RAM+12MB as the minimum, and doubled as the maximum. So in this instance, the minimum should be 44MB and the maximum should be 88MB.

24 A. *Run RDISK.EXE from the command prompt.* Running RDISK.EXE will update or create your Emergency Repair Disk.

25 D. *Log off and log back on using the VGA mode option, then remove the offending driver.* After you log back on to the Windows NT environment, the Last Known Good option is no longer a valid solution. It will only work if you have not completed your logon. Also, if the screen is totally unreadable, going to the command prompt to remove the video driver would be impossible. The only correct answer is to boot your computer into VGA mode to successfully remove the offending driver.

26 B. *In the Client Service for NetWare, check the Notify When Printed option.* In the Client Server for NetWare window, you have three printing options available: Add Form Feed, Notify When Printed, and Print Banner.

27 C. *Nbtstat.* Nbtstat is a command line utility that can used to gain configuration and statistical information about NetBIOS over TCP/IP in a TCP/IP network.

28 B. *The solution produces the required result only.* Proxy Server can provide Internet access and security for a network, but IP Forwarding allows Proxy Server to pass all IP traffic from the Internet into the LAN — a serious security breach.

29 *B. Fault Tolerance.* A mirror set, which is a fault-tolerant solution, can be configured via Disk Administrator's Fault Tolerance menu.

30 *C. DLC.* The Data Link Control protocol is a nonroutable protocol often used to provide communication with Hewlett-Packard printers, but it can also be used to communicate with IBM mainframe computers.

31 *C. Event Viewer.* You can view STOP errors, as well as information about warnings and general system events that occur, by using Event Viewer.

32 *D. $.* You can make any share a "hidden" share by adding a dollar sign ($) to the share name.

33 *A. 255.0.0.0.* The default subnet mask of a Class A network is 255.0.0.0. A Class B network is 255.255.0.0, and a Class C network is 255.255.255.0.

34 *A. DiskPerf -Y.* The DisPerf -Y command enables your computer to view both logical and physical disk counters remotely, which are not available by default.

35 *B. 10Base5.* 10Base5 can provide cable lengths up to 500 meters before a repeater must be used.

36 *D. Log off and log back on.* Whenever user permissions are changed on the NT Server, the user must log off and log back on for the changes to take effect.

37 *B and D.* Incorrect Desktop and Color Palette settings can cause Windows NT to display a blank screen when you test the new settings.

38 *A. Broadcast.* Routers do not pass broadcast messages to other network segments, and thus provide an effective means for reducing the possibility of broadcast storms.

39 *B. #PRE.* All entries in an LMHOSTS file with the #PRE are loaded into the name cache.

40 *A. Single Master Domain.* When you have smaller groups of users in multiple departments, and you want to centralize accounts but decentralize resources, the Single Master Domain is the best option.

41 *C. Click the Obtain an IP address from a DHCP server button.* A DHCP Server can automatically assign IP addresses to clients. To use this option, click the Obtain an IP address from a DHCP server button.

42 *B. $1/4$.* When you create a stripe set with parity with four disks, one-fourth of the total drive storage space is used for the parity bit. If you use three disks, one-third of the drive space is used for parity.

43 *D. Virtual Private Network.* PPTP enables the creation of a VPN so LAN traffic can be routed over the Internet to remote segments.

44 *D. DNS.* Domain Name System (DNS) is a static record that resolves domain names to IP addresses.

45 *B. The permissions of the target folder.* When copying a folder to another NTFS partition, the copy inherits the permissions of the target folder.

46 *B. 3.* To implement disk striping with parity, a fault-tolerant solution, at least three disks are required.

47 *A. Advanced Cable Tester.* Advanced Cable Testers work at the Physical layer of the OSI model and can gather beaconing information as well as frame count and collision information.

48 *B. This Computer Only.* To restrict TCP/IP clients from using the entire network, select the This Computer Only radio button. This option restricts the clients to the RAS Server.

49 *B. Run the emergency repair process by booting from the setup disks.* If an NT Workstation will not boot properly, you probably have corruption in one or more of the boot files. You can repair the boot files by booting from the NT setup disks and running the emergency repair process.

50 *A. WINS.* The Windows Internet Naming Service (WINS) translates NetBIOS, or computer names, to IP addresses for communication on a TCP/IP network.

Index

Notes

Notes

Notes

Notes

Notes

Notes

Notes

Notes

Notes

Notes

Notes

Notes

Notes

Notes

Notes

Notes

Notes

Notes

"Upset? Why should I be upset? So I couldn't reschedule my exam this weekend and still had to show up at precisely 8:00 Monday morning. And so what if it took till 10:39 before it was finally ready for me to take it. Does that bother me? Noooooooooo. I'm just going to sit right here and drink my nice lovely cup of tea!"

Hint: Now is not a good time to tell him he should have tested at a VUE Authorized Testing Center.

With VUE's real-time web-interface you can register or reschedule your exam 24 hours / 7 days a week, not just when someone happens to be answering the phone. Also, all VUE Testing Centers are tied into our powerful registration system, so you can register and pay at the site, and be taking your exam minutes later. And if you want to take another crack at an exam that you just 'sub-optimized', a VUE testing center should have your exam ready in less than five minutes.

Also, VUE is the only testing network that live-links your records directly with Microsoft and Novell's certification databases; you can test at any VUE Testing Center with the assurance and confidence that your results will get where they need to go.

To register for a Microsoft exam call toll free 888-837-8616 (USA & CAN), to register on the Web or to obtain a complete list of world-wide toll free phone numbers go to www.vue.com/ms

When it really matters, test with VUE.

Microsoft Certified
Professional
Exam Provider

VUE ®

VIRTUAL UNIVERSITY ENTERPRISES

a division of  NCS ®

**For more information, go to
w w w . v u e . c o m**

©1998 NCS, Inc. All rights reserved.

Discover Dummies™ Online!

The *Dummies* Web Site is your fun and friendly online resource for the latest information about *...For Dummies*® books on all your favorite topics. From cars to computers, wine to Windows, and investing to the Internet, we've got a shelf full of *...For Dummies* books waiting for you!

Ten Fun and Useful Things You Can Do at www.dummies.com

1. Register this book and win!
2. Find and buy the *...For Dummies* books you want online.
3. Get ten great *Dummies Tips*™ every week.
4. Chat with your favorite *...For Dummies* authors.
5. Subscribe free to *The Dummies Dispatch*™ newsletter.
6. Enter our sweepstakes and win cool stuff.
7. Send a free cartoon postcard to a friend.
8. Download free software.
9. Sample a book before you buy.
10. Talk to us. Make comments, ask questions, and get answers!

Jump online to these ten fun and useful things at
http://www.dummies.com/10useful

For other technology titles from IDG Books Worldwide, go to
www.idgbooks.com

Not online yet? It's easy to get started with *The Internet For Dummies*®, 5th Edition, or *Dummies 101*®: *The Internet For Windows*® 98, available at local retailers everywhere.

Find other *...For Dummies* books on these topics:
Business • Careers • Databases • Food & Beverages • Games • Gardening • Graphics • Hardware
Health & Fitness • Internet and the World Wide Web • Networking • Office Suites
Operating Systems • Personal Finance • Pets • Programming • Recreation • Sports
Spreadsheets • Teacher Resources • Test Prep • Word Processing

IDG BOOKS WORLDWIDE
BOOK REGISTRATION

We want to hear from you!

Visit **http://my2cents.dummies.com** to register this book and tell us how you liked it!

✔ Get entered in our monthly prize giveaway.

✔ Give us feedback about this book — tell us what you like best, what you like least, or maybe what you'd like to ask the author and us to change!

✔ Let us know any other ...*For Dummies*® topics that interest you.

Your feedback helps us determine what books to publish, tells us what coverage to add as we revise our books, and lets us know whether we're meeting your needs as a ...*For Dummies* reader. You're our most valuable resource, and what you have to say is important to us!

Not on the Web yet? It's easy to get started with *Dummies 101*®: *The Internet For Windows*® *98* or *The Internet For Dummies*®, 5th Edition, at local retailers everywhere.

Or let us know what you think by sending us a letter at the following address:

...*For Dummies* Book Registration
Dummies Press
7260 Shadeland Station, Suite 100
Indianapolis, IN 46256-3945
Fax 317-596-5498

BESTSELLING
BOOK SERIES
FROM IDG